FERRARI
TURBOS
The Grand Prix Cars
1981-88

Anthony Pritchard
Photographs by Nigel Snowdon

ASTON PUBLICATIONS
Sole distributors for the USA
Motorbooks International
Publishers & Wholesalers Inc.

Published in 1989 by
Aston Publications Limited
Bourne End House, Harvest Hill
Bourne End, Bucks, SL8 5JJ

ISBN 0 946627 50 9

Designed by Chris Hand

Printed in Hong Kong

Sole distributors to the UK book trade
Springfield Books Limited
Norman Road, Denby Dale
Huddersfield
West Yorkshire, HD8 8TH

Sole distributors in the United States
Motorbooks International
729 Prospect Avenue, Osceola
Wisconsin 54020
United States

CONTENTS

Author's Note

This is an illustrated history of the Ferrari turbocharged Grand Prix cars during that exciting period of racing, 1981-88 with, hopefully, a comprehensive record of their development, their racing performances and the successes and failures of their drivers. There is however an untold story. During this fascinating period in racing, during which the power output of turbocharged engines almost doubled in five years, largely because of the use of Toluene-based fuels, which technically qualified as petrol, the supremacy of Ferrari, always something of a mythical quality, was shattered as Enzo Ferrari in his declining years interfered with the direction of the team without purpose and Maranello politics damaged the careers and reputations of drivers and engineers alike. For this untold story we shall have to await the revelations of Michele Alboreto, still one of the fastest and finest Grand Prix drivers in the world, despite his confidence-sapping years at Ferrari, and Stefan Johansson, whose talents were never fully recognised by either Ferrari or McLaren and whose Formula 1 career has slipped to the bottom of the ladder and unlikely to recover. Another one who in the fullness of time must tell his own story is Harvey Postlethwaite, now with Tyrrell as is Alboreto himself. They have much to tell and hopefully one day it may be published.

Nor can I pretend that this book gives a broad over view of racing as a whole during this era or of the development of the other cars. For details of McLaren, Williams and the other successful cars of the period, the reader is heartily referred to the *1000 BHP Grand Prix Cars* by Ian Bamsey (Haynes, 1988) and *Grand Prix Car Design & Technology in the 1980s* by Alan Henry (Hazelton 1988).

It is also of course sad to record that Enzo Ferrari himself died during the last year of the turbocharged era, an era in which he clearly believed that Ferrari could dominate, although it failed to do so.

Introduction

With the introduction of the 3000 cc Grand Prix Formula in 1966, there was also the alternative of a 1500 cc supercharged engine, but this route was not followed by constructors during the first ten years of the Formula. During 1966-67 racing was dominated to a substantial degree by the comparatively simple Repco-powered Brabhams, but in 1967 there had appeared the Ford-financed Cosworth V-8 that originally powered the Lotus 49 only, but was to become adopted by many constructors.

The Influence of Renault

Although, in addition to Ferrari and Ford, quite a number of other constructors built cars and engines to comply with the 3000 cc Formula, including Alfa Romeo (who also supplied engines to Brabham), B.R.M., Matra and Tecno, the one team to make a real impact with their Formula 1 engine was Renault.

In 1966 Renault had acquired Alpine, the Dieppe-based builder of specialist sports cars. During the 1960s Alpine had enjoyed a fair measure of success in the 1500 cc class of Prototype racing with well streamlined cars, using Renault-based engines and from those had developed the A-210 and A-220 3-litre V-8 Prototypes that achieved little, simply because they were so underpowered. By the middle of 1969 the Alpine team had withdrawn from racing. However they had not abandoned racing (anymore than Renault's present withdrawal of their own team from Formula 1 indicates a loss of interest in racing as such) and Renault decided to attack the problem of building a competitive car by following a different route. In 1974 there appeared the Alpine A-441 sports-racing car that dominated that year's European 2-litre Sports Car Championship. What was different about the Alpine

was that the 4-cylinder engine was turbocharged and the result was an engine infinitely more powerful than any of the opposition. The principles of turbocharging are discussed in Appendix 3. Careful development work achieved reliability to match the performance and after entering long-distance sports car racing in 1976, with initially disappointing results, the yellow-painted 2-litre A-442 won at Le Mans in 1978.

Renault also developed a Formula 1 single-seater, the RS01, that first appeared at Silverstone in 1977 driven by Jabouille and in 1978 the team again ran a single car for Jabouille. Once the Le Mans victory was under their belt, Renault concentrated all their efforts on Formula 1 and, as the turbocharged design was gradually refined and developed, with chassis improvements to match, became a serious force. Between 1980 and 1985 Renault won 14 Grands Prix and although they never won a World Championship, Renault driver Alain Prost was pipped by only two points by Nelson Piquet in 1983. Renault withdrew from racing at the end of 1985, under the compulsion of the Renault group's appalling financial losses and in the knowledge that the time for substantial success was past, without a completely new development programme.

Although Renault had never achieved the measure of success for which they had hoped, their influence on other constructors was immense and gradually there was a swing to the use of turbocharged engines. Eventually at the end of 1985 normally aspirated engines were banned altogether. FISA decided that the sheer power of the turbocharged cars must be checked. They were banned altogether at the end of 1988 (in which year the boost setting was limited to 2.5 bar) and replaced by the new Formula for normally aspirated cars up to 3500 cc. For two seasons, 1987-88 the turbos and the 'new breed' competed together on equal terms.

5

Ferrari

No one has tackled motor racing with greater fervour than Enzo Ferrari, who after racing the works Alfa Romeos under the banner of Scuderia Ferrari during the years 1930-1937, made sufficient money during the war years from his machine-tool business to set up afterwards as a constructor of racing cars. Ferrari chose the V-12 layout because ex-Alfa Romeo designer Giaocchino Colombo was available, because he could quickly design a V-12 inspired by his successful pre-war Alfa Romeo designs and because it was, rightly, believed that a V-12 would prove a bed-rock for future development. For Ferrari the Colombo 'short-block' V-12 was to be what, in their different ways, the XK engine was for Jaguar and the W.O. Bentley-designed LB6 was for Aston Martin.

Through competition success Ferrari was able to project the image that he was the natural successor to Alfa Romeo and that Ferrari carried the burden and responsibility for Italy's racing prestige. As Ferrari power developed, so grew the concept of the Ferrari 'family'. Ferrari's reputation for playing off one member of the team against the other, for interfering in team management, and for using melodramatic devices to influence the framing of the regulations and to raise finance, and Laura Ferrari's interference in the running of the company, are notorious. But this style of management is certainly not unique to Ferrari; it has characterized Italian business, politics and sports (witness the return to their home country from Italy of disillusioned British football players) and it is far from uncommon in the United Kingdom.

Ferrari has also suffered from the reputation of being slow to adopt new concepts and very much lacking the ability to innovate. Ferrari always believed that racing cars should be of strong construction and not only the sports-racing cars, designed for endurance racing, but also the Formula 1 cars were stronger and heavier than most of their rivals. Ferrari did not adapt disc brakes on a regular basis until 1959 (adopted by Jaguar in 1953 and by Vanwall in 1954). The first rear-engined Ferraris were not built until 1960 (Cooper had won their first Grands Prix with rear-engined cars in 1958) and did not build a monocoque car until 1964 (Chapman pioneered the monocoque structure in Formula 1 in 1962 with the Lotus 25).

However, as the years passed, so Ferrari did react more swiftly to contemporary design needs. For 1970 the team had adopted a flat-12 engine layout, unique in Formula 1 except for the Tecno which was an unsuccessful Ferrari clone. In its various forms the flat-12 achieved a great measure of success. Once Fiat had acquired its 50% shareholding in Ferrari, Ferrari no longer had any financial concerns and there was greater impetus to take on new ideas and concepts. When it was realised that the days of the flat-12 engine were numbered, work was put in hand on a successor. Like most teams, Ferrari were greatly influenced by the potential of the Renault turbocharged cars and this was the route that Maranello decided to follow at a very early stage. Along with the new British Toleman team, Ferrari, in 1981, were the first imitators of Renault.

1: *The Learning Curve, 1981*

Once Ferrari had determined to go ahead with the turbocharged car, progress was rapid; the first prototype was revealed at the Ferrari test circuit at Fiorano in June 1980, it ran in practice in the 1980 Italian Grand Prix at Imola and S.p.A. Ferrari S.E.F.A.C. relied on the cars throughout the 1981 season. It was, however, a season that started somewhat later than usual, with the first World Championship race, the US Grand Prix West, not being held until 15 March.

The reason for this was the protracted battle between FOCA (Formula One Constructor's Association) and FISA (Féderation Internationale du Sport Automobile). It was a power struggle between constructors and organizers which eventually ended in compromise. Racing had been plagued by the use of ground-effect sliding skirts, pioneered by the Lotus 78 of 1977. FISA had decided (and with the benefit of hindsight it was a very wise decision) that sliding skirts should be banned in 1981. However FOCA organized their own South African Grand Prix at Kyalami on 7 February. The race was supported only by the FOCA teams, that is the British teams, together with A.T.S., all users of the Ford-Cosworth engine, whilst the so-called FISA teams of Ferrari, Alfa Romeo, Renault, Talbot-Ligier and Osella all missed the race.

The result was a race in which every car was powered by the Ford-Cosworth engine, sliding skirts were allowed for the last time and for some while it was unknown whether the results of the race would count towards World Championship points. Although it was a successful, well organized event, with Reutemann at the wheel of his Williams FW07B winning from Piquet with the Brabham BT49, ultimately the race was not regarded as a World Championship event. Whilst the FOCA teams raced, the FISA teams had to be content with testing and development work, but this was probably to Ferrari's advantage because the new turbocharged cars needed all the development time that could be found.

Development of the new car was entrusted to Ferrari's Chief Engineer Mauro Forghieri. The engine was the work of long-serving engineers Franco Rocchi and Walter Salvarani, with assistance from Angiolino Marchetti.

The team decided upon a 120-degree V-6 engine, completely new in some respects but at the same time owing a great deal to previous Ferrari design practice. The team chose an 120-degree included angle between the two cylinder banks, very different from previous V-6 Ferraris, as this meant that there was plenty of space in the wide-angle vee for the turbochargers, fuel injection and electronic ignition. In addition the choice of a V-6, compared to a layout with a greater number of cylinders, meant that both crankshaft and camshafts were shorter and stronger. The twin overhead camshafts, four valves per cylinder and single-plug cylinder heads had been adopted from the team's practice with the flat-12 cars that had been raced until the end of 1980.

Construction of the engine was in light alloy throughout, with the twin overhead camshafts gear-driven from the nose of the crankshaft. Ferrari chose cylinder dimensions of 81 x 48.4 mm providing a capacity of 1496.43 cc. Fuel injection was by Lucas and Ferrari used the Magnetti Marelli 'Digiplex' electronic ignition system.

In developing the engine Ferrari had pursued two different paths, turbocharging and supercharging. Ferrari used KKK German-made turbochargers (the manufacturers were Kuhnle, Kopp und Kaush of Eperspach), exhaust-driven, with a compression ratio of 6.5:1. At this early stage of development, as always, there were very real doubts about the actual performance figures, but Ferrari quoted 545 bhp at 11,000 rpm which seemed distinctly modest and was only 30 bhp higher than the power output of the 1980 Tipo 312T5 cars.

The second route followed by Ferrari was the use of a Brown Boveri Comprex pressure-wave supercharger. The Comprex system had been developed by Brown Boveri mainly for use with diesel engines, but both this company and Ferrari believed that the system had substantial prospects for use in passenger cars, in addition to racing, and Ferrari signed an agreement with Brown Boveri for exclusive racing use of the system until the end of the 1981 season. The Comprex supercharger was mounted in the vee of the Ferrari engine, rather high, with a pressurized rotating drum, and with fresh air entering at one end, compressed by the pressure waves of the exhaust gases at the other and with the drum driven by a toothed belt from the engine. Although throttle response with the Comprex system was much superior to that of the KKK, power output was significantly less and the high mounting of the installation did little for the Ferrari's handling. In addition the KKK system generally proved more reliable.

The monocoque chassis was a riveted aluminium sheet structure, following on the lines of the 1980 Ferraris, but with a very strong internal frame. There was a single fuel cell at the rear of the monocoque. At the front the suspension was by lower wishbones, with fabricated upper rocking arms and at the rear there were fabricated upper rocking arms and wide-based lower wishbones. As usual, inboard coil spring/damper units were fitted front and rear. The engine was a fully stressed chassis member and the gearbox, a much stronger version of the transverse gearbox used in the 1980 car, with either five or six speeds, took the rear suspension loads. Unusually Ferrari opted to use Brembo disc brakes, from a company that had previously a reputation only in the motorcycle field, but were anxious to work with Ferrari in Formula 1, and these were mounted well clear of the underwing airflow and within the Speedline split-rim wheels. The bodywork consisted of a top section combined with the cockpit surround, a separate nose-cone and wing, engine cover and side pods, with the water radiator on the left and oil coolers on the right. Rather after the style of the 1980 T5 cars, there were large pod decks, with hot air exit ducts for the coolers.

It would perhaps be appropriate at this point to clarify the designation of the various turbocharged Ferraris. Ferrari insisted that the 'C' stood for *Corsa*, racing, and did not mean *Compressore*, supercharger, which seems a little odd. With the Comprex supercharger the model was originally known as the 126BBC but later this was changed to 126CX, whilst the KKK turbocharged version was known as the 126CK. Chassis numbers ran from 049, a continuation of the numbering series that had first started at the beginning of the 3-litre Grand Prix Formula in 1966.

After extensive testing at Fiorano, the prototype car, 049, appeared in practice at Imola in 1980 driven by Villeneuve. Already a number of changes had been made to the original design; the wheelbase had been lengthened by swept-forward front suspension arms (which also moved weight distribution more to the rear), the turbocharger intercoolers were now mounted vertically and there was a new engine cover, smoothly faired, whereas the original had something of a fin-shape to it. The car was also at this stage fitted with spring-loaded sliding skirts, for it was not until much later that it was known whether or not sliding skirts would be permitted in 1981. Ferrari had brought the 126C to Imola just to show that 1980 was not all gloom with the T5s, but that the fans had something to look forward to. Villeneuve lapped in 1 min 35.751 sec, and this time was accepted as his official practice time and gave him a place on the fourth row of the grid. At the end of January 1981 both Villeneuve and Pironi had lapped Fiorano in 1 min 1.20 sec with the Comprex-supercharged cars, the drivers were enthusiastic about the throttle response of this layout and it seemed likely that the cars at Long Beach would have Comprex superchargers.

Following Jody Scheckter's retirement from racing, Ferrari had brought into the team young French driver Didier Pironi. Pironi had driven for the Ligier team in 1980, had won the Belgian Grand Prix and he and the Ligier had on occasions in 1980 looked like an unbeatable combination. His driver pairing with Gilles Villeneuve looked immensely strong. Villeneuve, a man who has become a hero and legend, had immense enthusiasm and considerable intelligence, matched by oustanding natural ability; unfortunately from time to time his enthusiasm conquered his intelligence with unfortunate results. Despite all the immense promise of this very strong driver pairing, it was a team relationship destined to end in tragedy.

US Grand Prix West

By the first World Championship race, the United States Grand Prix West at Long Beach in California on 15 March, a number of further changes had been made to the 126Cs, mainly so far as the bodywork was concerned. There was now a much slimmer surround to the cockpit, there were re-profiled side pods with, on either side of the cockpit, three airfoil-section vanes and, behind them, smooth unbroken decking. To this race Ferrari brought both KKK and Comprex engines and the drivers practised extensively with both versions. On this slow street circuit, where throttle response was so vital, Brown Boveri were convinced that their engine installation would be used, but in fact the drivers found that they were far from happy with the Comprex superchargers.

The cars were readily distinguishable by their different exhaust notes; in contrast with the deeper note of the KKK, which was very similar to that of the Renaults, the Comprex cars were accompanied by a high-pitched whistle, not entirely dissimilar to that of a jet engine. Villeneuve complained that the Comprex engine had a bad flat spot at low revs through the hairpin bends and he was also plagued by a misfire during the final practice session with his KKK car. During practice the team had a total of three turbos blow. In addition Villeneuve was forced to use the spare car on the Friday because of a broken supercharger drive-belt on the Comprex car. What was only too clear was that the handling of the new cars was quite appalling, mainly because there had been insufficient chassis development (the team had concentrated almost entirely on the engines) but there was no problem with their straight-line speed. Villeneuve was fifth fastest in 1 min 20.462 sec, whilst Pironi was 11th fastest in 1 min 20. 909 sec.

When the starting light turned green, Villeneuve, using the full power of the turbocharged engine, accelerated through the grid to pull out a lead of close to 50 yards, only to reach the first hairpin bend much too quickly, braking hard and sliding wide, so that he slipped back again to fourth place, with Pironi sixth. When Villeneuve's engine hesitated, both Pironi and Piquet (Brabham) slipped ahead. On lap 18 Piquet went ahead of Pironi whilst Villeneuve made his way to the pits to retire because of a broken half-shaft. Pironi dropped further and further behind Piquet, because of fuel starvation, which developed into a turbocharger problem, and he eventually retired on lap 68 of this 80-lap race.

Brazilian Grand Prix

From Long Beach all the teams flew directly to Brazil for the next race in the Championship series. Although there were few opportunities for the teams to make any changes to the cars, the Ferraris had now adopted side pods with side vents and unbroken top decks, something previously tested, but perhaps more significantly both Williams and Brabham were experimenting with suspension lowering systems as a means of circumventing the ban on sliding skirts. The Comprex-supercharged cars appeared in practice in both Brazil and Argentine, but were not raced and after these two events Ferrari relied exclusively upon the KKK turbochargers.

The Brazilian race was run on the Rio Centro Autodromo, a 3.126-mile circuit set in the sandy wastelands some dozen miles south of Rio de Janeiro and used previously for a Formula 1 race only once in 1978. The only real problem with this circuit was a liberal dusty, sandy coating which meant that the drivers were in real trouble if they strayed off the line cleared by the cars, into this sandy mess. So far as the Ferraris were concerned, both were suffering from only too obvious handling problems. Villeneuve commented that the Ferraris were around 15 kph faster than the Cosworth-powered cars along the straight but lost it all through the corners. Driving at his very hardest, a delight to watch despite the shortcomings of the car, Villeneuve was seventh fastest in 1 min 37.497 sec (compared with the 1 min 35.079 sec of pole-position man Piquet). Pironi tried hard, too hard, went off line into the dust on the Saturday morning and badly damaged his race car.

An hour before the race, rain started to fall and in fact became progressively heavier during the race. The race proved a complete shambles. Pole-position man Piquet elected to run on slicks, believing the circuit would dry out, and at the start Villeneuve accelerated into the back of Prost's slow-starting Renault, Andretti (Alfa Romeo) hit the back of the Ferrari and rose into the air crashing down and in addition to Andretti, both Arnoux (Renault) and Serra (Fittipaldi) were eliminated on the spot. Villeneuve pressed on, the front nose-wing askew, holding seventh place before calling into the pits for a new nose-cone. During the pit stop the mechanics fitted slick tyres, another mistake, but in any event he retired on lap 25 because of a broken turbocharger wastegate. Pironi's car had also made a pit stop when slicks were fitted and on lap 20 when Pironi moved over to let through Prost's Renault, he hit a puddle, slid into the Renault, and both cars were eliminated. The race was dominated by the Williams FW07Cs of Reutemann and Jones which took the first two places.

Argentine Grand Prix

The teams now moved on to Buenos Aires for the Argentine Grand Prix held on the municipal autodrome where Ferrari's efforts were largely overshadowed by major controversies affecting other teams. Reutemann had won in Brazil, apparently against team orders and the friction and rivalry between him and Jones was reaching its zenith, with local support very much on Reutemann's side; Brabham's hydro-pneumatic raising and lowering suspension system had been protested by Williams whose own system did not work(!); Colin Chapman was still fuming about the disqualification of his Lotus 88 'twin-chassis' car and had made a public statement that led to the imposition of a fine of $US 100,000 by FISA (to be rescinded after ten days). Villeneuve and Pironi got on with their quiet struggle with their ill-handling cars, with Villeneuve taking seventh place on the grid in 1 min 44.132 sec and Pironi back in 12th place in 1 min 45.108 sec (compared with Piquet's pole-position lap of 1 min 42.665 sec, a speed close to 130 mph). Nor did the race bring the team any joy. Villeneuve spun on the first lap, Pironi retired on only lap 3 with engine problems and Villeneuve fought his way back from the tail of the field, rising to tenth place before retiring with another broken drive-shaft on lap 40.

San Marino Grand Prix

This race at Imola, the second in Italy because the Italian authorities were able to argue tht by using the name San Marino it was the race of an independent republic, was another marred by scrutineering controversies. FISA was desperately trying to clarify its rules and make them beyond argument or dispute, but it seemed all that they managed to do was to thoroughly confuse the teams and their engineers. Despite protesting Brabham's hydro-pneumatic suspension system, Williams appeared at Imola with a similar system and the scrutineers ruled out both, together with systems fitted to cars from four other teams. Flexible skirts were also banned, as were the flexible end-plates on the nose-wings and the plates at the rear which at the rear which sealed the gaps between the ends of the side-pods and the rear wheels. Ferrari used fixed skirts and the only one of these decisions that affected them was the banning of the rear plates. To this race Ferrari had bought a new car, 052, for Villeneuve. This was the first of three cars to feature a number of modifications, inlcuding redesigned upper rocking arm pick-ups fabricated in titanium, an additional protective box-section ahead of the original pedal-box and revised skinning around the inboard coil spring/damper housings. This car also had a slightly longer wheelbase, as did Pironi's 051.

During Friday's practice a very clear pattern emerged; both drivers, with the boost turned up, were turning in dramatically quick laps and it was estimated that the Ferraris were now pushing out well over 600 bhp. Villeneuve set what looked as though it would be fastest lap of the session in 1 min 35.576 sec with the T car, the shorter wheelbase of which he preferred. This car was then taken over by Pironi, his own car having had engine trouble, but he was unable to improve on 1 min 36.168 sec. Shortly before the end of the session Arnoux with the Renault bettered Villeneuve's time with a lap in 1 min 35.281 sec, but the French-Canadian's efforts to regain pole position were destroyed by another broken turbocharger. During Saturday's practice Villeneuve was fastest in 1 min 34.523 sec, taking

The mechanics working on the 126C in the Ferrari garage at Imola in 1980.

pole position for the first time that year, and with Reutemann's Williams alongside him on the grid.

Race day again proved wet, with cooler weather which would favour the turbochargers. At the start of the race Villeneuve was slow away, but soon powered into the lead, whilst Pironi, who had managed to get a rolling start, accelerated through into second place. By lap 14 Villeneuve had realised that the track was drying out and that Alan Jones, whose Williams he had just lapped, was keeping pace with him, decided

Gilles Villeneuve impressed with the 126C on its first public appearance at Imola in 1980, lapping faster than with his T5, but deciding to drive the older car in the race.

upon a change of tyres and pulled into the pits for slicks to be fitted. No sooner was Villeneuve back in the race than heavy rain began to fall again and he had to make yet another pit stop. Villeneuve spent the rest of the race fighting his way back through the field and eventually finished seventh, two places behind Pironi. The Frenchman had battled to stay in front, despite a broken skirt and worn tyres, eventually losing the lead on lap 47 and gradually falling back down the field to finish fifth. A disappointing result after so much promise, but at least the turbocharged Ferrari had scored its first Championship points.

Belgian Grand Prix

A few day's before the Belgian race at Zolder FISA had issued a statement that hydraulic, pneumatic and similar springing systems were now officially permitted and skirts were to be solid. The result was that virtually all the teams, with exceptions of those of very limited means that could not afford trick suspension systems, were illegal, because whilst the cars all passed the necessary 6 cm ground clearance test in the pits, all were operating illegally out on the circuit. In addition because FISA had chosen not to use the word 'rigid', but 'solid', a number of teams had adopted rubber skirts.

Pironi's Ferrari, 052, was fitted with a hydraulic suspension system and with this he managed to record third fastest time in Friday's practice in 1 min 23.47 sec. Villeneuve, whose car had normal suspension, was seventh fastest in 1 min 23.94 sec. Both Ferraris ran with hydraulic suspension systems in the race.

At the start of the race which had been a disorganized shambles, Patrese's Arrows had stalled. Arrows' mechanic Dave Luckett went over the barrier with an airline to start the car, the grid moved off at the start and the other Arrows driver, young Siegfried Stohr, hit the rear of his team-mate's stricken car, trapping Luckett between the two cars. Fortunately the mechanic's injuries were relatively minor, but despite the fact that half the track was blocked, the organizers took no steps to stop the race. Eventually

the drivers themselves pulled off with, at that stage, Piquet leading from Reutemann.

The race was restarted after some 40 minutes, when Pironi screamed into the lead wiith Villeneuve in sixth place. As the race progressed so Pironi's brakes deteriorated. He was passed by Jones on lap 12, whilst further down the field Villeneuve was struggling; the hydraulic suspension of the Ferrari was not working properly, so that the nose of the car was permanently in the up position with the car showing a distinct reluctance to follow the direction dictated by the driver. The winner was Reutemann but both Ferraris finished, Villeneuve fourth and Pironi eighth.

Monaco Grand Prix

For the Monaco race, held on the most difficult, tight circuit in the series, with least opportunities for overtaking and likely to put the turbocharged Ferraris at a considerable disadvantage, Forghieri produced cars with much work having gone into the engines to improve the torque curve. Villeneuve was at the top of his form, pounding round the circuit in practice, using the immense power of the Ferrari wherever possible and combining it with his superb car control and reflexes to give the rather clumsy looking car second place on the starting grid with a time of 1 min 25.788 sec compared with Nelson Piquet's 1 min 25.710 sec with the Brabham. For Pironi it had all the makings of a thoroughly bad race. On the Thursday morning he crashed at the Rascasse corner and in the afternoon crashed the T car at Massenet, the curve leading into the Casino Square. Ferrari had to bring another spare car from the factory for Pironi to use. During the untimed session on Saturday Pironi's engine blew up, the only real engine problem suffered throughout the weekend by Ferrari, and he spun once more at Massenet with the spare car during the final hour of practice, flattening a rear tyre and damaging the rear bodwork and wing. He just managed to scrape in on the back of a grid with a time of 1 min 28.266 sec, and only three other qualifying cars were slower.

In the race Villeneuve initially held second place behind Piquet, was passed by Jones (Williams) and seemed to have settled for a steady third place. On lap 53 Piquet tried to lap Cheever's Theodore on the inside at Tabac, the front wheels locked on the dusty road surface and the Brabham slid into the barrier and out of the race. Villeneuve was now just over half a minute behind Jones, whilst as retirement followed retirement, Pironi was steadily making his way up the field and was now fourth. Believing that his engine was suffering from fuel vapourisation, Jones made a very brief pit stop to top up with fuel and by the time he was back in the race, Villeneuve was only six seconds in arrears. Although the Ferrari's brakes were fading, Jones' engine was still not running cleanly and on lap 72 Villeneuve accelerated past the Williams and into the lead as they approached Sainte Devote. Villeneuve went on to win the race by a margin of just over 20 seconds and Pironi finished fourth. For Ferrari it had been a magnificent triumph with their new car still not fully developed. Afterwards Villeneuve said that it had been one of the most tiring races of his life, mainly because the suspension was so stiff, the result of using the hydraulic system.

The French-Canadian was completely exhausted, complaining that his neck, arms and shoulders all ached badly.

Spanish Grand Prix

The Ferrari team arrived at Jarama for the Spanish Grand Prix with considerable optimism, whilst their rivals, mainly the British teams with non-turbocharged engines, viewed the future for themselves with some degree of despondency. There was no way they could match the sheer power of the Ferraris, and if Ferrari could evolve a half-decent chassis, then the Maranello cars would be completely unbeatable. For this race Ferrari brought along a new car, 053. The team did not run a T car, although they had brought 050 along.

Fastest in practice was Jacques Laffite with the Talbot-Ligier, with the two Williams cars of Jones and Reutemann close behind. Villeneuve was seventh fastest, whilst Pironi could manage no better than 13th. However, at the start Villeneuve was away like a rocket, pushing forward into third place, bending the nose-wing of Alain Prost's Renault. Into the first corner he passed Reutemann's Williams to take second, whilst Pironi was well placed in seventh spot. He too had had a minor collision, bending the nose-wing of his Ferrari as he pushed ahead of Patrese's Arrows. Despite all Villeneuve's talent, despite his flair

Two views of Gilles Villeneuve on his way to a win in the 1981 Spanish Grand Prix at Jarama.

Villeneuve after the Spanish Grand Prix, his sixth World Championship race win with a Ferrari — the first was in his home Grand Prix at Montreal in 1978.

and forceful driving, it seems very much as though the Ferrari's second place was a flash in the pan.

However on lap 14 Jones made a rare mistake, locking his brakes at the Ascari corner and rejoining way back in 16th place. Reutemann was trying to get past the Ferrari, but was having problems with his gearbox. Pironi was forced to stop at the pits for new tyres and a nose-cone. As the race progressed, so Villeneuve was hounded by Laffite's Ligier, Watson's McLaren, Reutemann's Williams and de Angelis' Lotus. On the straight the Ferrari pulled away from the opposition, and then baulked them through the corners. At the end of this 80-lap race Villeneuve was a mere one-fifth of a second ahead of Laffite, with Pironi at the tail of the field in 15th place, four laps in arrears. It had been an improbable victory, a victory of sheer horsepower, determined driving, of Villeneuve avoiding cockpit errors and making sure that there was absolutely no room for the other drivers through the overtaking lines into the slow corners.

French Grand Prix

From this point on during the year, the Ferrari drivers fought an unsuccessful battle with their unwieldy cars and were sometimes both trying too hard, sometimes both suffering from the most appalling misfortune and no further successes were

The Ferrari 126Cs lined up in front of the pits before the start of the 1981 French Grand Prix.

By the French race, the Ferraris had slipped back to mediocrity and Pironi's fifth place was a great disappointment after the team's wins at Monaco and Jarama.

gained. At the Dijon-Prenois circuit, scene of the French Grand Prix, the cars were overshadowed in both practice and the race. Villeneuve tried hard, so hard in practice, battling with the inadequacies of the 126CK and displaying true mastery in car control, but even he could only manage a time of 1 min 07.60 sec, 11th fastest, with Pironi three places slower on the grid in 1 min 08.09 sec. At this circuit, mainly thanks to their superior handling, the Renaults were in good form and pole position on the grid went to Arnoux in 1 min 05.95 sec. Villeneuve charged early in the race, rising to fourth place, but then gradually dropping back and seeming to show a lack of power out of the corners. On lap 41 he was out of the race when his electrics failed and the engine cut out. Pironi was back in tenth place. Heavy rain began to fall and the race was stopped during lap 59. After 30 minutes when the sun was shining again the remaining 22 laps were run and Pironi was classified fifth on the aggregate of the two races, one lap in arrears. The race was won by the Renault of Alain Prost.

Didier Pironi at the wheel of his Ferrari before the start of the 1981 French race.

British Grand Prix

In the days leading up to 18 July, the teams congregated at Silverstone for World Championship, Round 9, the British Grand Prix. Ferrari brought along a new car, 054, for Villeneuve, but he also had as a spare the so-called 051B. These B-specification cars, rebuilds of the first to appear, featured a new completely enclosed scuttle structure round the dash panel roll-over bar, sheet fillets either side of the cockpit opening to stiffen the chassis, a new nose-crush structure to the full depth of the monocoque and the front rocking arm pick-up was faired into the monocoque by sheet metal. Practice was dominated by the Renaults which took the first two places, Arnoux leading Prost in both sessions with Pironi finishing fourth on the grid with a time of 1 min 12.644 sec compared to Arnoux' 1 min 11.00 sec and Villeneuve trailing in eighth place in 1 min 13.311 sec. For both Ferrari drivers the race was soon over at Silverstone. The Ferraris were well away at the start and although Prost's Renault led at the end of the first lap, Pironi was second and Villeneuve third, leading the second Renault of Arnoux. It was not to last however, for at the chicane at Woodcote

The start of the 1981 British Grand Prix, with the turbocharged Renaults accelerating into the lead.

Villeneuve held fifth place at the end of lap 3 in the British Grand Prix, but on the following lap he crashed. He tried to struggle back to the pits with his damaged car, but was obliged to abandon it out on the circuit.

Although John Watson was at the peak of his form at this time, there was a strong element of luck in his win at Silverstone with the McLaren MP4.

at the end of lap 4, Villeneuve clipped the kerb on the left-hand swerve in the middle of the chicane, bounced off, caught the kerb on the right-hand swerve at the exit and spun. Hidden in a vast cloud of tyre smoke, the Ferrari was rammed by Jones' Williams and the two cars ended up in the catch fencing. With battered nose and bodywork and two punctured tyres, Villeneuve set off round the course again eventually being forced to abandon the Ferrari at Stowe Corner. Pironi was driving steadily, moving up to third place on lap 12, but on lap 14 the Ferrari was out with engine failure. The race was won by John Watson at the wheel of his McLaren, with Reutemann (Williams) and Laffite (Talbot-Ligier) taking second and third places.

German Grand Prix

After the British Grand Prix, the various designers involved in Formula 1 agreed between them, and this included Mauro Forghieri of Ferrari, that the hydralic ride height control equipment should be thrown away and the current Formula 1 weight limit should be reduced by an equivalent amount. It seemed that many of the problems of Formula 1 could be solved, especially that of rock-hard go-kart suspensions, and the ability to use softer suspensions would have suited Ferrari perhaps more than any other team. However it was Enzo Ferrari,

Didier Pironi's 126C in the pit lane at the 1981 United States Grand Prix West. This was race debut for the turbocharged Ferrari.

1981

17

Gilles Villeneuve, the most exciting driver of the 1980s, a hero in his time and now a legend.

French driver Didier Pironi was always overshadowed by Villeneuve's brilliance and this led to an intense and tragic rivalry.

Engineer Mauro Forghieri was a long-term member of the Ferrari team and the chief architect of its successes and failures. He is now with Lamborghini and responsible for that team's new Formula 1 engine.

Villeneuve in action at Long Beach during practice. He retired in the race because of drive-shaft failure.

Pironi with his 126C in the 1981 Monaco Grand Prix. The race was won by team-mate Villeneuve.

Gilles Villeneuve scored his second successive race victory in the 1981 Spanish Grand Prix at Jarama.

Didier Pironi at the wheel of his 126C at the Dutch Grand Prix at Zandvoort.

Villeneuve in the rain-soaked 1981 Canadian Grand Prix on the Ile Notre Dame circuit at Montreal. This

through the words of Marco Piccinini, who said that there seemed no good reason why the existing weight limit should be changed.

At Hockenheim Renault were again dominant in practice with Ferrari struggling. Whilst pole-position man Alain Prost lapped in 1 min 47.50 sec, Pironi was back on the third row of the grid, fifth fastest in 1 min 49.00 sec with Villeneuve a row further back in 1 min 49.44 sec. Both cars were running in the slightly longer wheelbase form, going like dingbats on the straight and suffering the most terrible handling horrors through the curves. In addition the team suffered two engine blow-ups during practice, one each by Pironi and Villeneuve. The race was another disaster for the team, for Pironi retired with engine trouble on the second lap and after holding sixth place in the opening laps, Villeneuve gradually slid down the field to finish tenth. The race was won by Nelson Piquet (Brabham).

Austrian Grand Prix

Ferrari was still struggling, not altogether convincingly, to improve the handing of the cars, because it seemed in fact they were waiting until a new design was ready for 1982. However, in Austria both cars had revised suspension geometry front and rear, reprofiled side pods and the rear suspension was now held by a dural plate instead of the former magnesium alloy casting. During Friday's practice Pironi crashed, and after his Ferrari had been repaired, he found that it was pulling to the left badly. On the Saturday he had a turbocharger failure, but he eventually managed to qualify eighth with a lap in 1 min 34.871 sec. Villeneuve was third fastest, on only his fifth lap, in 1 min 33.334 sec, compared with pole-man Arnoux' 1 min 32.018 sec. On Villeneuve's sixth lap the turbocharger blew.

In the German Grand Prix race Villeneuve was again out of luck and finished tenth, slowed by an engine misfire.

The winner at Hockenheim was Nelson Piquet with a Cosworth-powered Brabham BT49C and Piquet was to win the World Championship by the margin of one point from Carlos Reutemann (Williams).

Once again Villeneuve made a brilliant start, accelerating through from the second row and managing to hold on to a lead for the whole of the first lap. On only the second lap the Ferrari refused to respond to the steering at the Hella Licht and slid down the escape road, with Villeneuve rejoining the race in sixth place. Only ten laps later Villeneuve went

In Austria Ferrari adopted a single dural mounting plate for the rear suspension in an effort to improve handling.

off at the Boschkurve, rebounding from the guard rail across the track, but able to crawl back to the pits to retire. Pironi had been in third place, holding up several of the unblown cars through the corners and falling further and further behind second-place man Arnoux. Eventually Laffite forced his way past with his Ligier, and as the race progressed, Pironi slowed by a damaged skirt and ineffective brakes, dropped back to finish ninth, a lap in arrears.

Dutch Grand Prix

By the Zandvoort race the Ferraris were showing all signs of progressing backwards. For some reason that the Ferrari engineers could not fathom, the engines were down on power and during practice Pironi suffered a very frightening crash. During the first session on the Friday morning the front wheels became airborne at Scheivlak, a downhill right-hand bend with a bad bump, and the Ferrari slithered through the grass and into the catch fencing. The screen of the Ferrari was torn away by a pole which hit Pironi's helmet. Undoubtedly Pironi had the better engine but he could only manage 12th fastest in practice and Villeneuve was back in 16th place. For both Ferrari drivers the race was soon over for

The Austrian race proved another disappointment for Villeneuve and he crashed his 126C on lap 12 at the Boschkurve, mainly because of inadequate brakes.

A lovely overhead shot of Villeneuve in the pits at Zandvoort in 1981.

Villeneuve was out on the first lap after a collision with Giacomelli's Alfa Romeo and Pironi brought his Ferrari into the pits at the end of that first lap because of steering damaged in a collision with Tambay's Ligier. Didier rejoined the race, but the car was handling so badly there was no alternative but for it to be withdrawn. The race was won by Prost (Renault).

Italian Grand Prix

For the Monza race, on Ferrari's home territory and so important to the team, Maranello made almost desperate efforts to get the cars competitive, including two days' testing which had produced some encouraging lap times. Forghieri considered that the main problem with the car was the skirts, which wore too quickly through contact with the track and this drastically affected the handling of the cars. So at Monza new skirts appeared, which it was hoped would prove more durable. It was all to little avail.

First lap scramble at Monza in 1981 — without a Ferrari in sight.

The Italian Grand Prix was won by Alain Prost with his Renault RE30, the make that started the turbocharged revolution.

The best Ferrari performer at Monza was Didier Pironi who finished fifth, on the same lap as the winner.

During Friday's practice Pironi crashed at the exit of the 150 mph second Lesmo curve, writing off the left-hand side of the car, but fortunately escaping with only a bruised rib. He was soon out again in the T car, but was unhappy with it because of a vibration, returned to the pits and was allowed out in Villeneuve's T car. When Villeneuve retired to the pits with a blown engine, desperate to get out in the T car, he was horrified to find that Forghieri had let Pironi take it out. Villeneuve, stuck with a blown engine and a completely unused set of tyres with no car to put them on, seethed with anger, complaining vociferously to the Ferrari team and press alike, it was an early sign in the breadown of relationships between Villeneuve and Pironi. Pironi was marginally faster in practice, eighth in 1 min 35.596 sec, whilst Villeneuve was ninth fastest in 1 min 35.627 sec. Rene Arnoux took pole in 1 min 33.467 sec with his Renault.

When the cars were lined up on the grid, Pironi had his Ferrari positioned more towards the middle of the road than to its proper position on the right, so that on the green, he was able to accelerate through, passing Watson and Piquet, on the approach to Lesmo he passed Arnoux, then took Reutemann and completed the first lap in second place. After only six laps Villeneuve, who had not made as good a start as usual, was out with a blown turbocharger. Once again, as the race progressed, Pironi slowly fell down the field and eventually finished fifth. Villeneuve's misery over the weekend was rounded off when he went to his helicopter after

the race to fly back to Monte Carlo. The aircraft had been broken into, the radio equipment stolen, and he was stranded in Milan.

Canadian Grand Prix

There was a bare fortnight between Monza and Montreal in which to sort out the ravages of the Italian race, and in fact the teams were arriving in Canada only seven day's after the Italian Grand Prix. The Ferraris were still struggling, and during Saturday's practice Villeneuve crashed at the first turn after the pits, the car taking off completely, getting right off line and hitting the kerb at the next corner before rebounding back into the air, bending the suspension and tearing off the nose-section. Certainly, Villeneuve was trying too hard, but the real problem was the rock-hard suspension, coupled with the inherent handling shortcomings of the Ferrari, rather than any real problem in the cockpit. Both drivers were well back on the grid, Villeneuve in 11th place in 1 min 31.115 sec and Pironi, 12th in 1 min 31.350 sec. On the Sunday, when the race started, the circuit was being lashed by heavy rain and it was clearly going to be a thoroughly miserable and slow race. On the first lap, Villeneuve, trying to pass Arnoux' Renault, bounced into the back of the French car and pushed it into Pironi's Ferrari and out of the race with bent suspension. By lap 15 Villeneuve was in second place behind Lafitte's Ligier

Gilles Villeneuve (left) and Didier Pironi before the 1981 Canadian Grand Prix. Pironi was always overshadowed by his more talented team-mate.

with Watson (McLaren) sitting behind the Ferrari and waiting for a chance to pass.

Pironi moved up into fourth place, but on only lap 24 his Ferrari blew its engine and the Frenchman was out of the race. Watson was pushing Villeneuve closer and closer, eventually slipping past on lap 38 as they went into the first chicane and then the French-Canadian collided with de Angelis' Lotus at

the hairpin and both cars spun off. With battered nose and a worsening engine misfire, Villeneuve plugged on, eventually finishing third behind Laffite and Watson.

In the rain-soaked Canadian race Villeneuve collided with de Angelis' Lotus 87 when in second place. He carried on with nose askew and the front aerofoil later broke off completely. Because of an engine misfire Villeneuve eventually dropped back to finish third.

Las Vegas Grand Prix

From Montreal the Formula 1 teams took a 2500-mile journey in 16 trucks to Caesar's Palace, Las Vegas — and four of the trucks broke down on the way! The Las Vegas Grand Prix was a landmark in Formula 1 of the worst kind. The track had been formed in and around the car park of Caesar's Palace Hotel which overshadowed the circuit, with a lap distance of 2.26 miles, and a most peculiarly tortuous configuration, incorporating three very tight infield loops with limited run-off areas. Some limited assistance for the turbocharged cars came from the fact that the circuit had an elevation of 2200 ft above sea level, as altitude obviously favoured them. Once again, by a combination of sheer guts, sheer determination and fantastic car control, Villeneuve achieved third place on the grid with a time of 1 min 18.060 sec, compared with pole-position man Ruetemann's 1 min 17.821 sec. Again Pironi was

overshadowed; he was disappointing throughout practice in his Ferrari, a few laps before the end of the final practice session his turbocharger blew and when he took over the T car, he found that there were fuel injection problems. He ended up in 18th position on the grid with a time of 1 min 19.899 sec.

At the start Villeneuve moved into second place behind Jones (Williams), with a pack of hounding cars striving to pass him, but it was to prove to no avail. Villeneuve had been excluded from the race because at the start he had allowed the Ferrari to roll outside the starting box painted on the track. Villeneuve was not shown the black flag and raced on until lap 22 when he pulled off the road with the rear of the Ferrari ablaze. Pironi took ninth place, two laps in arrears.

For Ferrari it had been a season of immense promise and immense disappointment, but much was to change for 1982 which was to prove both a tragic and successful year.

2: *Triumph and Tragedy, 1982*

During 1981 Ferrari had possessed the best pair of drivers, together with the most powerful engine in Formula 1, but now he had the means to produce a chassis to match the other qualities of the team. During 1981 Dr. Harvey Postlethwaite, former designer with Hesketh, Wolf and Fittipaldi, joined Ferrari. Although Postlethwaite was convinced that the way forward was to build a carbon-fibre composite chassis, he also was convinced that on the basis of existing Ferrari experience and facilities, this was not the immediate solution. Accordingly he elected to design a honeycomb sheet chassis. Much of Postlethwaite's initial period at Maranello was spent setting up facilities for the manufacture of these monocoques. Ferrari worked closely with Hexcel, an American concern whose European subsidiary was based in Belgium; this company supplied materials and, in particular the honeycomb sheet, for initially

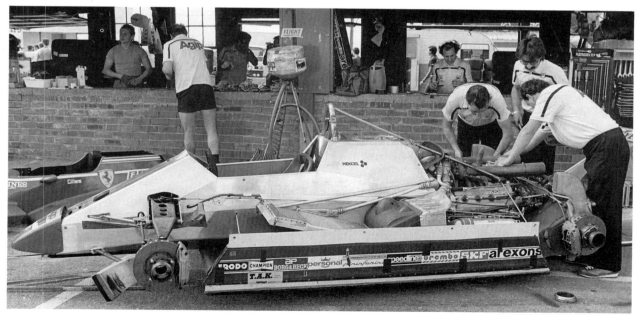

The new 126C2 cars made their debut at the 1982 South African Grand Prix.

Ferrari had no resin bonding facilities.

The basic design of the 1982 Ferrari followed closely that of the 1978 Wolf, for which Postlethwaite had been responsible, with two thin sheets of aluminium sandwiching the internal foil honeycomb and these panels folded into channel sections round carbon-fibre composite bulkheads and bonded down the centre-line. Although the monocoque was generally similar in shape to that of the 1981 Ferraris, it was lower and of course lighter than its predecessor. The sides of the cockpit were higher and blended into the dash panel surrounds and the foot box structure in the nose. Generally the lines of the car, in particular the nose, were smoother.

There were many detailed changes to the engines and because there was now a forward sloping rear bulkhead behind the fuel tank cell, the turbochargers could be moved further forward. Ferrari concentrated purely on the KKK turbocharged engines. Again, although the suspension closely followed the 1981 layout, there were minor changes and overall the cars looked much smoother and neater than their predecessors, especially at the rear where panelling enclosed the lower part of the engine and extended round the transmission casing. Another — and significant — change was that after four years Ferrari had switched from Michelin to Goodyear tyres. In addition FISA had now banned hydro-pneumatic suspension systems and all that was permitted were 6 cm fixed skirts that could be attached to the side panels and rubbing strips. This meant that the ground clearance checks in the pit lane, a too familiar sight in 1981 were no longer to be a feature of the Grand Prix scene and, in addition, the Formula 1 weight limit had been reduced from 585 kg to 580 kg.

South African Grand Prix

To the South African race Ferrari brought two cars, 055 for Villeneuve and 056 for Pironi. The turbocharged opposition now came from Brabham (with B.M.W. engines) as well as Renault and Toleman. Most teams had already tested extensively at Kyalami, so it was not such a desperate blow when the first practice session on the Thursday was abandoned because of a drivers' strike arising from the wording of the super-licence contract issued by FISA. Pironi was a leading light in this drivers' revolt. The dispute was eventually sorted out and the cars all appeared for practice on the Friday. Despite all the winter's work, the Ferraris were still not to the fore and Villeneuve turned in 1 min 07.106 sec, third fastest, with Pironi on the third row with a time of 1 min 8.360 sec. Fastest of all was Arnoux with the turbocharged Renault in 1 min 06.351 sec. Nor did the Ferraris fare well in the race. Villeneuve was eliminated on lap 7 by turbocharger failure after holding third place, and after a tyre change and plagued by an engine misfire Pironi finished in 18th and last place.

Front and rear suspension, largely unchanged from the 1981 cars with rocker arms operating inboard-mounted coil spring/damper units front and rear.

Brazilian Grand Prix

Soon after Kyalami, Pironi had a bad crash at the Ricard-Castellet circuit during a testing session. The throttle had jammed open, the Ferrari shot off the track, through the catch fencing, over a barrier and a bank, and into a spectator fence. Bruised knee apart, Pironi was unhurt, but his car, 055, was completely destroyed. Because of the number of crashes suffered by the Ferraris during the year, Maranello spent much of the season simply building replacement cars. For the Brazilian race the team provided Pironi with 056, the car that he had driven in South Africa, whilst there was a new chassis, 057, for Villeneuve.

Villeneuve was second fastest in practice (1 min 29.173 sec against pole-man Prost with the Renault in 1 min 28.808 sec) and Pironi, struggling, took eighth place on the grid in 1 min 30.655 sec. Villeneuve once again accelerated into the lead at the start, while Pironi held sixth place, but on lap 3 he spun off and rejoined the race back in 16th position. Villeneuve held his lead for 29 laps, hounded by Piquet (Brabham) and Rosberg (Williams) but on lap 30 he took a right-hand bend a little too tight, ran wide, found it difficult to turn on the power outside the racing line, and Piquet was alongside as they went into the next left-hand bend; as he endeavoured to fight off the Brabham, Villeneuve put two wheels off the edge, locked the brakes, and ploughed across the track and into the barrier. The race was now Piquet's. Pironi finished in eighth place, a lap in arrears.

Subsequently, both Piquet and Rosberg who finished second, were disqualified because their cars were fitted with water tanks for the water-cooled braking systems which needed topping up after the race in order to comply with the minimum weight regulations at post-race scrutineering. It was all part of a ploy to make the non-turbo cars more competitive, and it was Renault that protested the results. As a result, third-place man Prost (Renault) was elevated to winner, and Pironi rose to sixth place in the official results.

United States Grand Prix West

A number of changes had been made to the Long Beach circuit since 1982, mainly because of major construction work in the town itself. These included a chicane with a concealed entry on the fastest part of the circuit, and this led to a long left-hand corner which was to form the pit lane entrance in 1983. This chicane restricted the power benefit of the turbo cars when they should have been going at

Although the Ferraris were still disappointing in Brazil and whilst Villeneuve retired, Pironi could only finish eighth on the road, but was elevated to sixth place after the disqualification of Piquet (Brabham) and Rosberg (Williams).

Villeneuve's 126C2 with the staggered wing that was to lead to his disqualification from third place in the 1982 United States Grand Prix West.

their fastest. Remarkably, Andrea de Cesaris (Alfa Romeo) took pole position in practice, while Villeneuve was back in seventh place on the grid and Pironi was only ninth fastest. For this race there was a new car, 058, for Villeneuve. During Saturday's untimed practice session Forghieri had fitted Villeneuve's car with a very wide staggered two-piece wing. At the time it was written off as being a joke, aimed at the British teams and their many devices to circumvent the regulations. If it was a joke, then it was to prove a costly joke. Rear wing width was governed by the regulation limiting coachwork behind the rear wheels to 110 cm. What Ferrari had done was to use

two 110 cm wings staggered, with the right-hand wing ahead of the left-hand. Although the total width of the wings exceeded the regulation width, each wing in itself was apparently legal.

By Villeneuve's standards, it was a boring race. De Cesaris led initially, with Villeneuve back in fifth place, but a collision between Arnoux (Renault) and Giacomelli (Alfa Romeo) on lap 6 elevated him to third place. Eventually Lauda (McLaren) pulled ahead of de Cesaris, Rosberg passed Villeneuve, and so when de Cesaris retired after hitting a wall, Villeneuve was still third, and that was where he finished.

However, on a protest entered by Tyrrell, Villeneuve was disqualified because of the allegedly illegal rear wing, Pironi had a poor race, retiring on lap 7 after hitting a wall and bending a lower wishbone when in ninth place.

San Marino Grand Prix

Because of the disqualification of Piquet and Rosberg from the Brazilian race, and because of the decision by FISA to ban the topping up of liquids and coolants before post-race scrutineering, most of the FOCA teams withdrew from the Imola race. This left as starters only a field of 14 that included Ferrari, Alfa Romeo, Renault, together with Tyrrell (because they had just negotiated a three-race sponsorship from the Italian Candy washing machine company), A.T.S., Osella and Toleman. In practice the Renaults of Arnoux and Prost were fastest, with Villeneuve and Pironi on the second row. It was not a practice session without problems, however, because of the Friday afternoon Pironi crashed, for reasons not entirely clear, but possibly because of a puncture, destroying his 126C2 against the armco.

Initially Arnoux led the race, hounded by Villeneuve and Pironi, but first Villeneuve went ahead to take the lead on lap 27, three laps later he was relegated to second place and then was passed by team mate Pironi. Arnoux led until lap 45 of this 60-lap race when he was eliminated by engine failure. With the Ferraris now holding first and second places, the Ferrari pits showed 'slow' signals and there was every likelihood that the remainder of the race would

The battle for the lead in the San Marino Grand Prix with Villeneuve leading Pironi who passed him (more than once!) against team orders and won the race. After San Marino Villeneuve never again spoke to Pironi.

prove a mere procession. However only a lap later Pironi had taken the lead, but Pironi was only putting on a show for the crowd, surely? For after all the Ferrari arrangement was that the 'slow' signal meant the drivers should keep station and in any case the Ferraris were marginal on fuel in this race. Pironi led at the end of the next three laps, but then Villeneuve went ahead again for the next four laps, significantly reducing lap speeds, whilst Pironi, who went in front again on lap 53, was clearly driving his hardest and working desperately to stay in front. There was another swap of the lead on lap 59 when Villeneuve went ahead again, but Pironi snatched the lead once more on the last lap to win by less than a second. For Pironi it was a fine victory, but for Villeneuve Pironi's driving represented a breach of trust and honesty. Villeneuve, quite rightly, believed that Pironi had stolen the race from him against team orders. He had every reason to be angry with the Frenchman, but his anger went just a little too far and his vow never to speak to Pironi again was too extreme in its seriousness; it was a vow he maintained until his own tragic death which was to occur a mere 13 days later.

Belgian Grand Prix

To the Belgian Grand Prix on the rather dreary Zolder circuit, Ferrari brought along 058 for Villeneuve and a new car, 059 for Pironi. Both cars featured strengthened lower rear suspension members.

Since the accidents in the pit lane and on the grid itself in 1981, the whole of the existing pits structure had been demolished, and there was a new and vastly improved pits complex with wide access road and wide apron in front of the pits themselves.

Throughout practice there was a taut, edgy atmosphere in the Ferrari team as Villeneuve implemented his vow not to speak to Pironi. On Friday neither car went as well as the team had hoped and Villeneuve's best lap in 1 min 17.507 sec was only fifth fastest, whilst Pironi was out of the picture because of electrical trouble. The Frenchman was slightly faster on the Saturday and this merely spurred Villeneuve to greater efforts. Shortly before

the end of practice, on what would have been his last lap, he collided with Jochen Mass' March, the Ferrari cartwheeled across the track, the nose dug into the sand, and the French-Canadian, his neck already broken, was flung out of the cockpit as the Ferrari flew on. Practice was stopped immediately, and Villeneuve rushed to hospital. The consequences of the accident were only too clear and the Ferrari team packed up to go home. Villeneuve died that evening.

Undoubtedly the most exciting driver of his generation, with a potential still not fulfilled, and with an enthusiastic following that few other drivers have been able to achieve, Villeneuve's death was not just a tragedy in itself, but a tragedy because of his breakdown of relations with Pironi, a tragedy for Ferrari and motor racing; for some while it seemed that the team would not be able to readily recover from this terrible blow. In the absence of the Ferrari team the winner at Zolder was John Watson (McLaren).

Because the Ferrari's chassis had apparently disintegrated there was much criticism of Postlethwaite's design methods, for it was claimed that the aluminium honeycomb system of very thin skins resulted in a structure that could tear and split under heavy impact. Ferrari carried out extensive static rig tests on two of the monocoques, one of the latest cars, and a original 1981 car. Postlethwaite — and Ferrari — satisfied themselves that the structure of the Ferrari was more than adequately strong and that the accident had been exceptional in every respect.

The accident was investigated by a FISA enquiry commission which, amongst other things, confirmed that the survival cell of the Ferrari fulfilled its role and stated, 'The cause of the accident was attributed to driver error on the part of Gilles Villeneuve. No blame was attached to Jochen Mass'. Whilst these words are undeniably true, they did tend to skate round the problems that had caused the accident. The pressures on Villeneuve were immense, not only because of his determination to prove through action rather than words that he was a superior driver to Pironi, but the pressure on him to turn in a really fast time on what was his last lap on qualifying tyres. The accident would have been avoided if Villeneuve had

Didier Pironi in practice for the Belgian Grand Prix, from which the Ferrari team withdrew after Villeneuve's fatal crash.

backed off when he met Mass' March at this critical point on the circuit, but everything in Villeneuve's nature compelled him to believe that it was a situation that he could control — and he nearly did.

Monaco Grand Prix

Ferrari left the decision to run at Monaco to Pironi who chose to race. Maranello provided two cars, 059, together with 056, now completely rebuilt, as a spare. Pironi qualified fifth fastest in 1 min 24.585 sec and for much of the race over the street circuit held third place behind Prost (Renault) and Patrese (Brabham). Ten laps before the finish, light rain began to fall, the circuit became exceptionally greasy and a mere two laps from the finish Prost lost control at the exit from the chicane along the waterfront and ploughed into the armco. So slippery was the circuit that on the same lap Patrese lost his Brabham on the approach to the Station hairpin on the penultimate lap, letting Pironi into the lead with a lap and a half to go.

On the very last lap the Ferrari's engine died in the tunnel because of electrical failure. Patrese rejoined the race to take the chequered flag and Pironi was classified second, a lap in arrears.

Pironi at the wheel of his 126C2 at Monaco in 1982. Here and in the next two races he was the sole Ferrari entry.

United States Grand Prix (Detroit)

While Ferrari was casting around for a new driver to join the team, Pironi struggled on as the single Maranello entry, appearing at the Detroit race with 059 and 056 as a spare. 056 had now been modified by fitting pull-rod front suspension, inspired by Brabham practice whereby there were inboard coil spring/damper units acuated by lightweight pull-rods

Despite the fact that his car expired in the tunnel with electrical trouble on the final lap, Pironi was classified second at Monaco. The car lost its nose-cone in a collision with de Angelis' Lotus.

and with rocker links replacing the top rocker arms. These changes transformed the handling of the 126Cs, for a with a lighter front end and smaller frontal area, there was reduced tyre wear and much improved steering into corners. Although Pironi used the new car to set fourth fastest practice time in 1 min 49.903 sec, he used the car with the original front suspension in the race.

In the opening laps Prost (Renault) led. Pironi moved up to third place on lap 4, but only two laps later the race was stopped after a collision between Guerrero (Ensign) and de Angelis (Lotus) which also involved Patrese's Brabham. Over an hour later the race was restarted and Pironi again held third place, behind Prost and Rosberg, but then Prost was passed by Rosberg and when the Renault pulled into the pits

Pironi in practice for the Detroit Grand Prix in which he finished third, a good performance by a solo entry.

with a faulty fuel injection pump, Pironi moved up into second place. The race was stopped at the end of two hours (instead of the original planned 70 laps) and Pironi was third behind the winning McLaren of Watson and Cheever's Talbot-Ligier.

Canadian Grand Prix

In memory of Gilles Villeneuve, the Île Notre Dame circuit at Montreal had been renamed the Circuit Gilles Villeneuve and the teams met there a week later for the Canadian Grand Prix. At this circuit Pironi raced 056 fitted with pull-rod suspension and in practice he was the fastest in 1 min 27.509 sec.

This race was marred by yet another appalling tragedy. Partly because of the long delay between Pironi arriving on the grid to take up his pole position and the red light being shown that the start was imminent, the Ferrari crept forward on the clutch, Pironi touched the brake to hold the car in place, and the engine died just as the green light came on. With his engine stalled, Pironi raised his left arm in warning. Other drivers dodged round the stricken car but Boesel (March) struck the Ferrari a glancing blow and then Riccardo Paletti, with his Osella, accelerating hard from the back of the grid, completely unsighted, ran straight into the back of the Ferrari. The impact punched the Ferrari to the left of the track where it collided with the Theodore of Geoff Lees. The race was stopped immediately, Pironi was out of the Ferrari and assisting as quickly as possible, while the medical team were on the scene within a matter of seconds. Fuel from the ruptured tank of the Osella caught alight, and as the medical team worked, efforts were made to control the fire. Paletti was eventually cut free, without any burns, but he died a few hours later from major internal injuries.

When the race restarted, Pironi was at the wheel of his training car, without pull-rod suspension, with all its inherent handling problems, and although he led at the end of the first lap, he gradually fell further and further down the field stopping at the pits for fuel and new tyres, and then again for adjustment of the fuel metering system and replacement of the

black box, rejoining the race to eventually finish ninth. Nelson Piquet scored a victory with the B.M.W.-powered Brabham.

During testing at Paul Ricard, Pironi suffered yet another crash, apparently caused by a broken suspension wishbone, and, although the car had ended up a write-off in an empty spectator enclosure, Pironi was unhurt. It was this failure that led to the use of strengthened wishbones at Zandvoort.

Patrick Tambay at the wheel of a 126C2 at a test session at Brands Hatch shortly after he had signed up with Ferrari.

Dutch Grand Prix

By the Zandvoort race, Patrick Tambay had joined the team. Tambay's last Formula 1 drive had been in 1981. He had been nominated as substitute driver in South Africa in 1982 after Marc Surer had a testing crash with the Arrows, but withdrew, weary of the wranglings of Formula 1, after the drivers' dispute. His instructions at Zandvoort were to play himself in gently. Although Pironi could only manage fourth fastest time in practice in 1 min 15.825 sec, on lap 5 of the race he moved up from third place to take the lead ahead of Prost (Renault) and Arnoux (Renault). With the Ferrari now handling superbly and well up on power, Pironi stayed in front to win by over 20 seconds from Piquet's Brabham-B.M.W.

A superb overhead view of Pironi's 126C2 in the pits at Zandvoort in 1982.

Tambay followed instructions and despite the fact that his Ferrari's engine refused to run cleanly, he finished eighth, a lap in arrears.

British Grand Prix

By the British race at Brands Hatch Ferrari had built another 126C2, chassis 061, which was driven by Tambay, while Pironi was again at the wheel of 060. On this very bumpy circuit the Ferraris failed to show the form expected, but were well up with most of the opposition. Rosberg took pole position with his Williams in 1 min 09.540 sec, with Pironi fourth fastest in 1 min 10.066 sec. Initially Piquet with the turbocharged Brabham-B.M.W. led from Niki Lauda (McLaren), with Pironi third, but when Piquet retired with fuel metering problems, Pironi moved up into second place, falling back to third again behind Warwick's Toleman. The Toleman was eliminated by failure of a constant velocity joint and so Pironi finished second, with Tambay coming through to take third place. Pironi now led the Drivers' Championship with 35 points to the 30 of John Watson.

French Grand Prix

Held on the very fast Paul Ricard circuit near Marseille, the French race proved to be a complete turbo benefit, and these cars occupied the first six places on the grid. Although the Renaults were fastest, in the final timed practice session, Tambay, running with a minimum amount of rear wing and the turbocharged boost turned up, achieved 215 mph through the speed trap on the Mistral straight. It was later claimed, without any real justification, that the practice engine used in Tambay's car was developing 720 bhp compared with Ferrari's official claim of 560 bhp. The best output from Renault and B.M.W. was reckoned to be 680 bhp and it was

Didier Pironi in practice for the British Grand Prix in which he finished second.

On his first race drive for the Ferrari team Tambay turned in a brilliant performance to score his first Grand Prix win and only Ferrari's second in 1982.

believed that all three teams' cars in race trim developed around 620 bhp. Throughout this period Ferrari had been experimenting with a longitudinal gearbox for the 126C2, but it was never raced because tests at the Fiorano test circuit had revealed that the necessary longer wheelbase to accommodate this gearbox adversely affected the weight distribution. Pironi tried the spare car with this gearbox during practice on each day, but settled for his regular car for the race, partly becaue he had spun into the catch fencing with the spare on the Saturday morning. Another Ferrari development at this time, in conjunction with AGIP, was a water-injection system whereby water droplets encapsulated within the petrol droplets, lowered the temperature of the petrol entering into the combustion chambers, and on combustion the water turned to steam, improving atomisation and mixture control. Not much was known about the system, save for the fact that there were grave doubts by the other teams as to its legality! It appeared to breach the regulation that banned fuel additives.

The Brabhams took the lead early in the French race, but first Patrese was eliminated by an engine fire and then Piquet dropped out with gudgeon pin failure. This left the two Renaults clearly in the lead and in this race that lasted little more than an hour and a half, they took first two places ahead of Pironi and Tambay.

German Grand Prix

In practice for the German race Pironi showed complete domination, taking pole by over a second on the Friday and, in torrential rain on the Saturday morning, easily fastest again. However, he completed only three laps before yet another terrible accident occurred, bringing the Frenchman's racing career to an end. One of the many problems caused by ground-effect racing cars was that on a wet circuit the spray was forced out from under the side pods as a fine mist and created virtually a fog. Pironi saw Derek Daly (Williams) move to the right on the straight and he believed that Daly was moving over to let him through. In fact Daly, acting quite properly, had

During Friday's practice for the German Grand Prix at Hockenheim Pironi took pole-position . . .

But the following day during wet practice Pironi crashed badly and suffered such severe injuries that he never raced again. Here his car is seen on the back of the rescue truck after recovery from the circuit.

In the race, however, all came good for Tambay and he scored a fine victory, 16 seconds ahead of Arnoux' Renault.

pulled out to the right to pass Prost's Renault which had slowed as it headed towards the pits. The left-hand front wheel of the Ferrari hit the rear wheel of the Renault, was launched into the air, somersaulted three times and came to rest against the guard rail. Pironi had suffered terrible leg injuries and it took over half-an-hour for him to be removed from the car. He was flown to Heidelberg University Hospital where major surgery was carried out. In addition to two breaks in his right leg, and the almost severing of his right foot, he suffered a broken left leg and arm, but no amputation proved necessary. It was obvious that Pironi was going to be out of racing for a very long time, if he ever returned at all, and although Ferrari promised to keep a place open for him in the team, he never did race again.

There now fell a tremendous burden on the shoulders of Patrick Tambay. He felt saddened, not only at Pironi's dreadful accident, but at the effect on the team and mechanics which had just begun to recover from Villeneuve's death and see success once more. Tambay had achieved fifth fastest practice time overall, elevated to fourth now that Pironi's pole position on the grid was left vacant and he had driven superbly and with immense confidence during the wet session.

Holding fourth place in the race initially, Tambay moved up to third, ahead of Prost (Renault); he passed Arnoux on lap 10 and moving into the lead on lap 19 when Piquet's Brabham, with a lead of 26 seconds, collided with Salazar's A.T.S. Now Tambay led a Grand Prix for the first time in his life, gradually

pulling out a 20-second lead and at the end of this 45-lap race he was 16 seconds ahead of Arnoux (Renault). The Frenchman had driven a magnificently controlled race in the most onerous of circumstances.

Austrian Grand Prix

At the Österreichring a week later, Tambay was fourth fastest in practice and his race was marred by misfortune. At the start the Alfa Romeos of de Cesaris and Giacomelli collided, and eliminated Daly's Williams. The track was cleared, but at the end of that first lap Tambay, holding fourth place behind the turbocharged Brabhams of Piquet and Patrese

Tambay's 126C2 at the Austrian Grand Prix.

Another view of Tambay's Ferrari, showing the engine installation.

and Prost's Renault, punctured a rear tyre on debris from the start line incident. This meant a long slow lap whilst Tambay struggled back, endeavouring to prevent damage to the suspenion and skirts, and eventually resuming two laps down after a wheel-change. As the race progressed, so Tambay gradually picked up places, and at the finish he was fourth behind the winning Lotus of de Angelis, Rosberg's Williams and Laffite's Talbot.

Swiss Grand Prix

Ever since the Le Mans disaster in 1955, motor racing has been banned in Switzerland, but that did not prevent the organization of a race of that name in 1982 on the Dijon-Prenois circuit. Again Ferrari entered only the one car for Tambay, 062, with 061 as spare. In Friday's practice Tambay was tenth fastest, but that night Tambay decided to give the final

qualifying session on the Saturday a miss so as to conserve himself for the race. Since the Wednesday after the Australian Grand Prix he had suffered pains in his neck, right shoulder and arm that gradually worsened, the result of a pinched nerve caused by the G-forces of modern racing and the rock-hard suspension. Tambay's pain increased throughout Saturday and on the morning of the race Ferrari announced the team's withdrawal. The race was won by Rosberg (Williams) from Prost (Renault) and Lauda (McLaren).

Italian Grand Prix

It was inevitable that the high speed Monza circuit would prove another turbo race and the turbocharged cars were to take the first three places. Tambay was fit enough to race again, and he was joined in the team by 42 year-old Italian-born American, Mario Andretti. Andretti, one of the world's most experienced drivers, had raced for Ferrari in 1971-2 and he had won the 1978 World Championship at the wheel of the Lotus 79. His last Formula 1 appearance had been at Long Beach in 1982 with a Williams. There Andretti felt that there had been insufficient time for testing and adjusting himself to the car and he retired after damaging the rear suspension of his Williams against a wall. For Monza he had made sure that there was adequate testing and preparation. Andretti was in his element, enjoying a reunion with Ferrari, with appreciation from the fans and with very real hopes of a great success. On the first day's practice, he was sixth fastest, but on the Saturday he took pole in 1 min 28.473 sec, with Tambay a strong third in 1 min 28.830 sec, the Ferraris split by Piquet with the turbocharged B.M.W.-powered Brabham. In the Ferrari pit there was real excitement, for on home ground, supported by their many thousand of enthusiasts, the Ferraris looked as though they were going to achieve victory.

During the warm-up, Tambay's Ferrari stopped with an engine problem. He had to rush back to the pits to take over the training car, but the original was repaired in time for the race. At the start Andretti

Left: Didier Pironi at the wheel of his 126C2 at the 1982 South African Grand Prix at Kyalami.

Below: Gilles Villeneuve in practice for the 1982 South African race from which he retired because of turbo failure.

Ferrari were out of luck again in the Brazilian Grand Prix. Here is Villeneuve who led until he spun into a guard-rail.

Villeneuve in the fateful 1982 San Marino Grand Prix in which he was beaten into second place by Pironi acting against team orders.

Gilles Villeneuve at the wheel of his Ferrari during practice for the 1982 Belgian Grand Prix. Shortly afterwards he was killed in an horrific accident, following a collision with Jochen Mass' March.

Below: Patrick Tambay, who came out of the wilderness to revitalise the Ferrari team and score a fine win at Hockenheim.

Above: For the Italian race at Monza and the Caesars Palace Grand Prix at Las Vegas the team was joined by Italian-born Mario Andretti, World Champion at the wheel of a Lotus in 1978.

Didier Pironi on his way to a win in the 1982 Dutch Grand Prix. It was to be his last victory for the Ferrari team.

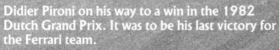

At the Italian Grand Prix at Monza the team was joined by Mario Andretti and despite a poor start he finished third behind team-mate Tambay.

made a dreadful mistake, letting the revs soar so that the rev limiter cut in and, with the time lost, at the end of that first lap Arnoux (Renault) led from Tambay and with Andretti back in fourth place. As the race progressed, it became only too obvious that Tambay had problems, which proved to be bad oversteer, whilst Andretti had a sticking throttle and Arnoux extended his lead more and more. As a race, it was but the blink of an eyelid, all over in 1 hour 22 min, with Arnoux leading home Tambay and Andretti. It was not what the enthusiasts wanted, but nevertheless it was a fine result and Ferrari was extending its lead in the Constructors' Cup.

Caesars Palace Grand Prix

Although it had been a long season with 16 Championship races, the final round, the Caesars Palace Grand Prix at Las Vegas on 25 September, was much earlier in the season than in most years. Ferrari sent along 062 for Tambay, while Andretti drove 061 and the new 063 was available as a spare. During qualifying for the race, both cars suffered from fuel vapourisation problems and their qualifying positions were seventh by Andretti in 1 min 17.921 sec and eighth by Tambay in 1 min 17.958 sec. Tambay was again very unwell, with a recurrence of the pinched nerve problem and was forced to withdraw from the race. Andretti was never in the running, holding sixth place initially, rising to fifth and then retiring on lap 27 when the Ferrari suddenly veered sideways; Andretti corrected and the car slid straight on into the sand because of broken suspension and a left-hand rear wheel that had taken charge of directional control. Suspension failure had been a problem all season, but in that final race it could cost Ferrari the Constructors' Cup in favour of McLaren. With their only driver out of the race, the Ferrari pit carefully watched the outcome. Victory went to Alboreto with his Tyrrell, leading home Watson's McLaren and Cheever's Talbot.

Ferrari took the Constructors' Cup with 74 points to the 69 of McLaren, with Renault trailing in third place with 62 points. Rosberg won the Drivers' Championship with 44 points, but Didier Pironi was still joint second with 39 points and the team's success was remarkable, bearing in mind that they had lost two drivers during the year.

3: *1983: A Second Constructors' Cup*

Although Harvey Postlethwaite was advanced with plans for the new 126C car with carbon-composite monocoque reinforced with Kevlar, this did not appear until the British Grand Prix at Silverstone in July. In the meanwhile Ferrari had built a test 126C3 prototype, using the existing 126C2 aluminium-honeycomb monocoque and with ground effects and the newly developed longitudinal trans-axle. In November 1982, however, the Formula 1 commission had, without consultation, banned ground-effect cars and now required that all cars featured a flat under-body within the wheelbase. The test hack was scrapped and in the early part of the 1983 season Ferrari raced the existing 126C2B cars in flat-bottom form and modified by the fitting of enormous rear aerofoils; the sides of the aerofoils extended to mountings on the rear of the side pods. Work had continued on engine development and the drivers had even more power at their disposal. Patrick Tambay remained with the team and he was joined by fellow-Frenchman René Arnoux, who had left Renault after a strained year in the team with Alain Prost.

At this point it would be appropriate to consider the opposition facing Ferrari in 1983. Brabham and A.T.S. (with B.M.W. engines), Renault, Alfa Romeo (whose turbocharged car had first appeared at Monza in 1982) and Lotus (with Renault engines, but initially fielding only one turbocharged car) were all turbocharged, together with the Hart-powered Tolemans (uncompetitive at this stage in their career), whilst Williams, Tyrrell, McLaren and the also-ran teams of March, Ligier, Arrows, Osella and Theodore all remained normally aspirated Ford-Cosworth users.

Ferrari's new signing for 1983 was René Arnoux, previously with Renault and seen here demonstrating gear-change and braking points on a plan of the Île Notre Dame circuit at Montreal.

Brazilian Grand Prix

At the first round of the World Championship on the Rio de Janeiro Autodromo, the Ferraris were never in contention for a win. Tambay was third fastest in practice in 1 min 34.758 sec, with Arnoux back in sixth place, slower than Warwick's Toleman. Neither driver was happy with either the engine or the handling of his car and the team faced very real problems with their Goodyear tyres. Tambay had held fourth place at one stage in the race, but dropped back to finish fifth, while Arnoux, plagued by vibration, the result of the Goodyear tyres moving on the rims, finished tenth. The race was won by Nelson Piquet's turbocharged Brabham.

United States West, Grand Prix

First held in 1976, the Long Beach Grand Prix was enjoying its last year. British ex-patriot creator of the event, Chris Pook, had concluded that the cost of staging the Grand Prix there each year was too high and had entered into a three-year agreement for the race to be held as a C.A.R.T. event. It had been a very popular street circuit, of great appeal and liked by drivers, but recently much of its character had been lost. A hotel had been constructed, which

meant that the uphill Pine Avenue, the fast Ocean Boulevard and the drop down Linden Avenue were gone, replaced by a succession of tight corners before the old circuit was rejoined. The pits had been repositioned along Shoreline Drive, which had a bad camber that made working on the cars difficult and with a sweeping curve that caused problems for signallers in the pits. Yet another problem was a bad bump at the bottom of Linden Avenue Hill, caused by subsidence in the road, at the point where drivers were about to brake heavily for the second-gear corner that followed. Immediately after Friday's practice, work started to cut out the bump and resurface.

In contrast to their performance in Brazil, the Ferraris were in peak form and Tambay (1 min 26.117 sec which he recorded on the Saturday) and Arnoux (1 min 26.935 sec) took first two places on the grid. Quite why the Ferraris should be going so well was not at all clear, but undoubtedly the new rear wing had done much to improve traction.

Tambay took the lead at the fall of the flag, despite a slow start which had encouraged Rosberg to accelerate his Williams between the Ferraris, colliding with Arnoux' right-front wheel, bouncing over this Ferrari and spinning wildly; Rosberg carried on in third place, behind team-mate Laffite, with Arnoux fifth. Rosberg moved ahead of Laffite on the second lap and, out in front, Tambay, anxious to

For the first races of the year Ferrari adapted the 126C2 cars to comply with the new 'flat bottom' rule. Here Tambay is at the Brazilian race in which he finished fifth.

Patrick Tambay led the United States Grand Prix West with determination and style until punted out by Keke Rosberg (Williams) who was trying to snatch the lead. Here Tambay leads Rosberg shortly before the incident.

conserve his tyres, was setting his own pace, despite the hounding pack behind him. On lap 26 Tambay slid wide at the exit of the left-hand corner which led on to the short straight before the hairpin bend; Rosberg tried the inside line, the Ferrari's right rear wheel ran over the left front wheel of the Williams, the Ferrari jumped into the air and Tambay was out with a stalled engine. On the same lap Rosberg collided with Jarier's Ligier and both cars were eliminated. At the finish Watson and Lauda took first and second places with their McLarens, ahead of Arnoux' Ferrari which had made two pit stops for new tyres.

Race of Champions, Brands Hatch

Held over 40 laps of the Kent circuit, the Race of Champions on 10 April attracted only a small field of 13 cars, but did include the new Spirit Formula 1 car with Honda turbocharged engine. Ferrari sent a single 126C2B for René Arnoux, but the Frenchman was plagued by tyre problems and retired at just over half-distance because of engine failure. The race was won by the Williams of Keke Rosberg from Danny Sullivan's Tyrrell.

In the Race of Champions at Brands Hatch a sole 126C2 was entered for Arnoux, but it ran out of tyres and then retired because of engine problems.

French Grand Prix

One of the highlights of the 1983 season was refuelling stops. It had really begun with Brabham, whose B.M.W. engines were very marginal as far as fuel were concerned and who had devised the strategy of starting with a half-full tank and softer tyres, before making a pit stop to refuel and for new tyres, which more than compensated for the time lost in a stop — around 25 seconds. Rosberg (Williams) had made a stop in Brazil and whilst there was a flash fire during refuelling, nothing to do with the refuelling process itself, this did tend to highlight the dangers of refuelling stops. There had been talk of a ban on refuelling during a race but discussions led to nothing and eventually it was decided that refuelling stops would become banned in 1984. In the meanwhile both Ferrari and Renault decided to adopt this strategy. For the French race Ferrari had invested in sophisticated refuelling equipment that included aircraft-type couplings and the bill was said to top $10,000.

Held much earlier in the season than usual, at the Paul Ricard circuit well suited to turbocharged cars, Arnoux was fourth fastest in 1 min 39.115 sec (compared with pole position-man Prost (Renault) in 1 min 36.672 sec) and Tambay was back on the sixth row of the grid with a time of 1 min 40.393 sec. Once again all was not well with the Ferrari team, both drivers blew their turbochargers in practice and neither car was as fast as had been hoped for. In the race, dominated throughout by Prost (Renault) with Piquet soon moving up to second place, the Ferraris were never in the picture and Tambay and Arnoux finished fourth and seventh, a very disappointing performance.

San Marino Grand Prix

By the Imola race, turbocharged cars dominated the field and at the Italian circuit took the first ten places on the grid. The closing stages of practice witnessed a close battle between the turbocharged teams for pole position on the grid, but René Arnoux, almost remarkably, was fastest in 1 min 31.238 sec, just ahead of Piquet's Brabham and with Tambay in third place. At long last it seemed that the Ferrari team had got their act together and there were real prospects of a Maranello success on home territory.

Painted on the grid position to be occupied by

49

In the San Marino Grand Prix Tambay scored Ferrari's first victory of the year after Patrese's Brabham slid into a barrier shortly before the finish. This photograph was taken in practice.

Tambay's car, bearing racing number 27, the same as had been worn by the late Gilles Villeneuve, was a red and white maple leaf. It simply added to the burden of the Frenchman who was striving so hard to achieve success for the team which had still not recovered from the death of the French-Canadian.

Piquet made a poor start and Arnoux accelerated into the lead with Tambay third. When Arnoux stopped at the end of lap 20 for fuel and new tyres, Tambay moved up into second place behind Patrese (Brabham) and retained this position despite his own refuelling stop at the end of lap 32. Patrese stopped at the pits at the end of lap 37, but the stop was a complete shambles. He missed his mark for stopping, the car had to be pushed back and by the time he had rejoined the race, the Brabham driver was 10.6 sec behind Tambay. As the race progressed Patrese fought hard to close the gap on the Ferrari driver and Tambay was unable to fight back because of an engine misfire. On lap 55 Patrese took the lead, but crashed on the same lap. Tambay scored his first Ferrari victory of the year at an average

of 115. 251 mph from the Renault of Alain Prost with Arnoux in third place. The win put Ferrari into the lead in the Constructors' Cup, with 22 points, one point ahead of McLaren.

Monaco Grand Prix

Even at Monaco the turbocharged cars dominated. It had seemed that Arnoux would snatch pole, but this went to Prost with a brilliant 1 min 24.840 sec while Arnoux returned 1 min 25.182 sec for second place on the grid. Patrick Tambay was fourth fastest in 1 min 26.298 sec.

Shortly before the start of the race rain began to fall, and both the Renaults and the Ferraris started on wet tyres. Rosberg however opted for slicks. When the light turned green, Prost led away but Keke Rosberg with his Williams, fastest non-turbocharged driver in practice and fifth on the grid, had forced his way into the lead by the end of lap 2. On lap 3

René Arnoux and the 126C2 in the pits at Monaco in 1982.

It was fourth place for Tambay at Monaco and he would have finished higher but for poor team management. Tambay was kept circulating, waiting for a change from wet to dry tyres while the mechanics worked on Arnoux' shattered car.

Arnoux went off hitting the barrier at Portier. With the left rear rim and tyre damaged, Arnoux ground his way back to the pits, discarding tyre and metal on his way, and finally came to rest in the pit road. The Ferrari pit was the very first and so the mechanics were able to repair the car, and Arnoux eventually rejoined the race only to retire with electrical problems. Tambay, now in third place and losing ground, was kept waiting out on the circuit before he could come in and change to slicks and take advantage of the now drying road surface. He eventually stopped at the end of lap 10, rejoining the race in 11th place and gradually working his way up through the thinning field to finish fourth. Rosberg won the race from Piquet's Brabham. All in all an unsatisfactory performance by the Ferrari team, and the result could have been very different if Tambay had been able to pit earlier.

Belgian Grand Prix

At long last the Formula 1 teams returned to the wonderful circuit of Spa-Francorchamps set in the Ardennes, once the finest motor racing circuit in Europe, now reduced in length from 8.76 to 4.32 miles, but still maintaining much of its original character and magic, its fast sweeping curves and its spectacular scenery. The rebuilt circuit had been in use some years, for Formula 2 and Endurance racing, but once it was known that Formula 1 was to return, the paddock had to be redesigned and new pits were constructed before La Source hairpin bend.

On this high-speed circuit the Ferraris ran with smaller rear wings, and although not quite as quick as the fastest Renault of Prost, Tambay took second place on the grid in 2 min 04.626 sec. Arnoux was a little off the pace, fifth fastest in 2 min 05.737 sec.

At the start several drivers stalled, and although the red light had come on, this was followed by the flashing yellow light, meaning 'start delayed'. Both de Cesaris (Alfa Romeo) and Prost (Renault) somehow missed the flashing light and accelerated away. A second parade lap was held and two laps were taken off the race distance. Initially de Cesaris led from Prost, but the Alfa Romeo driver retired with engine trouble and Prost went on to score a fine victory. Starting in third place, with Arnoux fourth, Tambay drove a steady, but unspectacular race to finish second. Arnoux retired after 22 laps with engine trouble. The results meant that Ferrari had slipped to second place in the Constructors' Cup with 31 points to the 36 of Renault.

United States (Detroit) Grand Prix

Since the race had been held for the first time in 1982, a number of improvements had been made to the circuit and it was now much smoother, with many of the bumps ironed out. The first practice session was wet, but in the dry, warm session on the Saturday Arnoux took pole position in 1 min 44.734 sec and Tambay was third fastest. It had all the makings of a very successful race for Maranello. At the start Piquet, who had been second fastest, accelerated into the lead with his Brabham-B.M.W. but Arnoux took the lead on lap 10, while Tambay's race was over at the start; he stalled his engine on the grid and, instead of being given a push start, as he expected, the Ferrari was towed away and out of the race. Arnoux stayed in front until lap 31 when his car expired because of a broken electrical wire. Piquet seemed set for a certain victory, running through the race non-stop, but on lap 51, the left-hand rear tyre punctured. He stopped at the pits for a wheel change and Alboreto took the lead to win with his Cosworth-powered Tyrrell.

Canadian Grand Prix

Ferrari almost, but not quite, dominated practice for the Canadian race on the Gilles Villeneuve circuit, with Arnoux taking a trouble-free pole position in 1 min 28.729 sec. Next came the Renault of Prost (1 min 28.830 sec) and the Brabham of Piquet (1 min 28.887 sec) and Tambay took fourth place in 1 min 28.992 sec. Tambay's practice had been far from trouble-free, for he had

found on the Friday that the car was bouncing badly and so the team tried stiffer springs on the Saturday, but without much improvement. That day the car also suffered a turbo failure. After switching to the training car, running on softer qualifying tyres, Tambay still could not improve on Friday's time.

Arnoux led almost throughout the race, gradually extending a lead over Patrese, but dropping back to fourth place after his pit stop at the end of lap 35. By lap 39 he was in front once more, Patrese retired with gearbox problems and at the finish Arnoux led Cheever's Renault by 42 seconds. It was a well deserved victory, for it had been his third pole position during the 1983 season and his form had steadily been improving. Tambay drove a steady race to finish third.

British Grand Prix

Over a month had elapsed between the Canadian and British races and this gave Ferrari the time to have the new C3 cars ready for the Silverstone race. The C3s first appeared in a tyre testing session at Silverstone in late June. The monocoque of the C3 was a carbon-fibre composite constructed in its entirety at Maranello and 'cured' in the giant oven which had been installed within the competition department; this monocoque was a single structure which incorporated the nose-cone, the cockpit surround and fuel cell, formed in two main sections and bonded together. The engine, gearbox and suspension came straight of the C2B. Ferrari had for the time being abandoned plans to use the longitudinal gearbox. When tested at Silverstone in June the cars featured abbreviated side pods, but by the time they were raced, the longer side pods from the C2Bs had been fitted because oil overheating had been experienced.

At the Grand Prix the cars ran with smaller centre-pillar rear aerofoils. In practice the Ferraris dominated, with Arnoux fastest in 1 min 09.462 sec, and Tambay alongside him on the grid in 1 min 10.104 sec. The Ferraris led initially, Tambay ahead of Arnoux, but the new aerofoils gave insufficient downforce and, with reduced grip from their tyres,

At the British Grand Prix at Silverstone the new 126C3 car was raced for the first time. Here is Tambay in the pits. Although the Ferraris led early in the race, smaller aerofoils and reduced downforce resulted in blistered tyres and Tambay and Arnoux fell back to finish third and fifth.

the Ferraris were sliding badly and blistered their rear tyres. By the end of the race they had dropped back, Tambay finishing third and Arnoux fifth, with victory going to Alain Prost (Renault) and with Piquet (Brabham) in second place. A disappointing end to what in practice and the early laps of the race had shown all the signs of a Ferrari domination to be.

At Silverstone Ken Tyrrell protested the legality of the water injection system used by both Renault and Ferrari. Tyrrell alleged that water injection constituted a power boosting additive contravening the regulations, whereas Ferrari claimed that it was purely for cooling the air intake charge. There was a lot of sound reasoning behind Tyrrell's protest, but apart from the fact that it simply introduced more disharmony into Formula 1, it did Tyrrell very little good, for the French Elf concern who had been supplying fuel to Tyrrell for many years, took grave exception to his protest at Renault (whom they also supplied) and withdrew supplies from the British team. Eventually the protest was settled in Ferrari's and Renault's favour.

German Grand Prix

By the race at the Hockenheimring Ferrari had reverted to the larger aerofoils used prior to Silverstone and in addition had made a number of changes to the bodywork of the C3 cars to reduce weight. The team was now once more in magnificent form and Tambay was fastest in practice in 1 min 49.328 sec, with Arnoux alongside him on the grid. Tambay led initially, but then Arnoux pushed ahead while Patrick was content to hold second place. Tambay's car started to run rough, he made a stop for plugs on lap 11 and retired on the following lap. Apart from seven laps, when Piquet led after Arnoux had stopped for fuel, the surviving Ferrari driver led

René Arnoux in practice for the German Grand Prix which he won with the 126C3 car after passing Tambay against team orders.

throughout and at the finish was 1 min 10 sec ahead of de Cesaris' Alfa Romeo. Ferrari had now regained the lead in the Constructors' Cup with 59 points to the 56 of Renault.

Austrian Grand Prix

At their third successive race the Ferrari team took pole position and at the Österreichring Tambay was fastest in 1 min 29.871 sec, with Arnoux alongside him on the grid in 1 min 29.935 sec. Although there were problems further back on the grid, both Tambay and Arnoux made a perfect start and settled down to hold a Ferrari procession at the front of the field, a sight to delight the enthusiasts who had crossed the border from Italy to watch the race. On lap 22 Tambay caught Jarier (Ligier) on the approach to the Glatzkurve. Jarier, instead of giving way to the race leader, held his line and continued to block him on the approach to the Boschkurve by taking a very tight line at the exit of the curve, Arnoux boxed Tambay behind the Ligier and went into the lead and Piquet shot through to take second place.

Arnoux stopped at the pit at the end of the lap 28, Tambay was fighting back and squeezed past Piquet at the exit to the chicane. It was clear however

At the Österreichring Arnoux reinforced his position in the Ferrari team by finishing second, albeit only after passing Tambay by boxing him in behind a slower car.

that the Ferrari would not last the distance for it was laying a haze of oil and retired at the end of lap 30 with engine trouble. Arnoux fought back after his pit stop, but was unable to pass Piquet until the Brazilian's Brabham lost power and the Ferrari went ahead again. Only six laps from the finish, Arnoux ran into problems with his gearbox and whilst he was struggling to get into fourth, Prost took the lead and victory with his Renault. At the finish Arnoux was just under seven seconds behind the French car. In the Drivers' Championship Arnoux had scored 34 points, compared with the 51 of Prost and the 37 of Piquet, while Tambay's total was 31. Renault once more led the Constructors' Cup with 68 points to the 65 of Ferrari.

Dutch Grand Prix

Centre of attention at Zandvoort was the new McLaren with the T.A.G.-Porsche turbocharged engine, driven by Niki Lauda. Destined in the fullness of time to dominate racing, at Zandvoort the new car showed immense promise, but not yet race-winning potential. Lauda was well back on the grid with a time of 1 min 20.169 sec, but ran well in the race until eliminated by brake problems. Fastest in practice was Piquet with his Brabham in 1 min 15.630 sec, but alongside him on the grid was Tambay in 1 min 16.370 sec, while Arnoux who suffered turbo failure on the Friday and ignition problems with his spare

Arnoux scored yet another victory in the Dutch race, but after clutch slip at the start of the race, Tambay came through to finish second.

After the Dutch race Arnoux celebrates his victory.

car, and completed only five practice laps in all, managed merely tenth place on the grid. The shifting of relations within the team was made only too clear because at this race the spare C3 car had been given to Arnoux, while Tambay had the older C2.

The start was delayed because the B.M.W. engine of Winkelhock's A.T.S. failed to fire when the field started their final parade lap. Tambay's clutch suffered badly and on the green light he almost stalled his Ferrari, eventually completing the first lap in 21st place and spending the whole of the race climbing back up through the field. From his poor starting position on the grid, Arnoux completed the first lap in seventh place, and he too gradually worked his way up through the field so that by lap 22 he was in third place behind Piquet (Brabham) and Prost (Renault). Arnoux made his pit stop at the end of lap 39, rejoining the race without losing his third place. On lap 41, Prost, trying to build up a good lead before his stop, took the inside line at Tarzan, the brakes locked on his Renault, and he slid into Piquet's Brabham which was pushed into the tyre barrier. Piquet was out, but Prost rejoined the race only to crash on the same lap when his Renault lost grip and slid hard into the barricade. Arnoux was now unchallenged in the lead and Tambay had moved up to third place. Tambay finished second after Patrese's Brabham had lost power. For Ferrari it had been a very lucky race, for although the cars had been fast and reliable, the odds had been very much against

Maranello at this circuit. Arnoux now held second place in the Drivers' Championship with 43 points to the 51 of Prost and Ferrari led the Constructors' Cup with 80 points to the 68 of Renault.

Italian Grand Prix

At Monza the Ferraris appeared with minor rear suspension modifications, but otherwise unchanged. Throughout the year the B.M.W. engines of the Brabhams had steadily been increasing in power and not only was Patrese fastest in practice in 1 min 29.122 sec, beating Tambay (1 min 29.650 sec) into second place on the grid, with Arnoux third in

Patrick Tambay at the wheel of his 126C3 at Monza.

1983

For 1983 Ferrari signed up René Arnoux, previously with the Renault team, and he stayed with Maranello for two and a half seasons and won two Grands Prix in 1983.

Arnoux with the updated 126C2 in the Brazilian Grand Prix in which he finished a poor tenth.

Forghieri confers
with Patrick
Tambay at the
1983 San Marino
Grand Prix.

At Imola, Tambay
was at the peak of
his form and scored
a fine victory in the
San Marino Grand
Prix with Arnoux
in third place.

René Arnoux in the Monaco Grand Prix in which he retired after an accident.

One of the best races of 1983 was the Italian Grand Prix in which Arnoux and Tambay took second and fourth places. Here Arnoux leads the Renault of Eddie Cheever.

1 min 29.901 sec and Piquet fourth in 1 min 30.202 sec, but the Brabham team led the entire race. Initially the order was Patrese – Piquet, but at the end of the third lap Patrese went out with engine problems. At the finish Piquet was a little over ten seconds ahead of Arnoux with Tambay, whose car had seemed down on power, back in fourth place. With a winning average of 135.178 mph, Monza was little more than a brief sprint and the race was all over in just over 1 hour 23 min. Prost still led the World Championship with 51 points, but Arnoux was only two points behind, and now Ferrari was breaking clear in the Constructors' Cup with 89 points to the 72 of Renault.

European Grand Prix

Originally in 1983 it had been planned that there would be a New York Grand Prix, but this was cancelled and so Britain was allowed a second round in the World Championship, the so-called European Grand Prix held at Brands Hatch. By now it was known that Michele Alboreto would be joining the Ferrari team in 1984, the first time that there had been an Italian driver in the team since 1973. Obviously either Arnoux or Tambay would be leaving Ferrari at the end of the year, and whilst Tambay had certainly been the more successful driver during the earlier part of the season, Arnoux had gone from strength to strength as the season progressed. This uncertainty did nothing to help the team's morale and everything about Ferrari at Brands Hatch seemed slightly lacklustre. De Angelis was fastest in practice with his Renault-powered Lotus. Both the Ferrari drivers were complaining of lack of grip with their Goodyear tyres and during practice Tambay had a nasty moment when his hand slipped off the roll bar adjuster on to the fire extinguisher – on came the fire extinguisher, off went the electrics as Tambay coasted towards Paddock Bend at around 170 mph with a dead engine and sprayed with extinguisher fluid, but managing to bring the car safely to rest. Arnoux and Tambay took fifth and sixth places on the grid.

For Ferrari it proved a disastrous race. By lap 20 Arnoux was in fifth place, behind Piquet, Prost, Patrese and Cheever, but already his tyres and brakes were beginning to give problems. At Surtees he spun the Ferrari, rolling backwards on to the outside of the circuit and rejoined the race after a push start. Whether Arnoux should have been disqualified for receiving outside help was an academic question, for after two pit stops and some indecision as to what tyres should be fitted, he finished well down the field in ninth place. Tambay too had more than his fair share of brake problems, but towards the end of the race he had worked his car up to third place, was passed by Mansell (Lotus) on lap 66 and two laps later was out of the race when the right front brake locked at Druids and the Ferrari spun into the barrier. Almost immediately Ferrari announced that it would be Arnoux who would be staying with the team in 1984.

South African Grand Prix

In reality Arnoux had lost all hope of winning the World Championship when he spun at Brands Hatch, but there was still a very slim chance that he could gain it by winning at Kyalami. Ferrari however was uncatchable in the Constructors' Cup. Tambay, in his final outing with the Ferrari team, took pole position in practice in 1 min 06.554 sec, with Piquet and Patrese splitting him from team-mate Arnoux (1 min 07.105 sec). During practice Arnoux' electrics had failed and whilst the Frenchman was trying to persuade the marshalls to push the car away from the dangerous position where it had coasted to a halt, a rear wheel ran over his right foot badly bruising it. The Brabham team dominated the race, whilst neither Ferrari ran well. Tambay was eliminated by ignition failure, and Arnoux driving in considerable pain, retired because a cracked cylinder head resulted in overheating. Patrese won the race for Brabham and, by finishing third with his Brabham, Piquet clinched the World Championship. For Ferrari, who had gained no points out of the last two races of the year, the Constructors' Cup was well deserved.

4: *1984: The Start of a Slow Decline*

In February 1984 Ferrari announced the new 126C4 car which was simply an updated version of the cars raced in 1983. The main changes to the car was that the upper section was stiffer, but the lower part of the monocoque was identical to that of the 1983 C3 cars. There had been reductions of weight in the engine and the gearbox and the cars also featured a very slightly lower centre of gravity. Arnoux remained with the team, but Michele Alboreto, who had learned the art of Grand Prix racing with Tyrrell and had won the United States Grand Prix at Detroit the previous June, had replaced Patrick Tambay. This move had disappointed many of the Ferrari team who had great confidence in Tambay's skill and sympathetic approach to racing. However, there was little to do apart from accept the fact that 'the old man' was greatly pleased to have an Italian back in the team again after many years.

Although Ferrari was to show good promise during the early part of the 1984 season, and to score an early victory in the Belgian Grand Prix at Zolder (which was to deceive Ferrari into believing the cars were now right), the year was to prove an almost complete benefit for the T.A.G.-powered McLarens which won every other race that year with the exception of three races, for the Canadian and Detroit races were won by Nelson Piquet with his B.M.W.-powered Brabham and the Dallas race which went to Williams (Rosberg).

Brazilian Grand Prix

In all Ferrari built nine C4 cars for 1984. The first chassis 070, was in reality a 1983 C3 car and used for development testing. The last chassis 078 was never completed. To most races the team took four cars and at the Rio de Janeiro circuit the team had 071 as a spare, whilst Alboreto drove 072 and Arnoux had 073.

It really did look as though Ferrari was to get off to a good start to the season, for Alboreto was second fastest in practice (to de Angelis' Lotus). Alboreto's car was running on Marelli/Weber electronic injection and management equipment, whilst in practice Arnoux whose car was fitted with Lucas injection was very much slower and far from happy with his car. He was back on the fifth row of the grid with a time 1.80 seconds slower than his team-mate. Alboreto made a magnificent start in the race and led until lap 12, steadily pulling out a lead until the end of that lap when his car suddenly spun; Alboreto got it all back together again, crossed the finishing line in third place, but immediately spun again and crawled round to the pits to retire the car because the front right brake caliper had broken, letting out all the fluid. Arnoux had steadily been pulling up the field after a poor start, and by lap 30 had risen to fifth place, but as he completed the next lap the Ferrari rolled to a halt because of battery

Newcomer to the team Alboreto with his Ferrari in the Brazilian Grand Prix. He led the race for 11 laps, but was eliminated by a broken front brake caliper that let out all the fluid.

failure. After Alboreto's retirement, Lauda had held a clear lead with his McLaren, but when he retired his team-mate Prost took the lead and went on to win the race from Rosberg's Williams.

South African Grand Prix

Following the failure at Rio de Janeiro, the Brembo company had modified the mountings of the brake calipers on the Ferraris. Alboreto again drove 072, whilst Arnoux was at the wheel of 073 and the team had 070 as a spare again. Maranello was expecting a very competitive performance at Kyalami from the Ferraris, but they were handling badly on the fast corners and after more wing had been adopted, they lost speed on the straight and the tyres blistered badly. There was some irony in the fact that the faster driver, Alboreto, was back on the fifth row of the grid, four rows behind Tambay with his Renault, and Arnoux who was on the eighth row, had failed to match the pole position set by Tambay in 1983. Neither car ran well in the race; Arnoux was

Michele Alboreto at the South African Grand Prix at Kyalami.

René Arnoux had a thoroughly miserable race at Kyalami and retired because of fuel injection problems.

eliminated by fuel injection problems and although Alboreto was classified 12th, five laps behind the winner, he was not running at the finish because of electronic ignition failure. Once again the McLarens dominated with Lauda and Prost taking the first two places ahead of Warwick's Renault.

Belgian Grand Prix

All came well at Zolder. Here, Alboreto drove the new car 074, while Arnoux retained 073 and the team had brought along 072 as a spare. Although the Ferraris were not on the pace during the first practice session, on the second day, with the boost turned right up, Alboreto set a new standard, with pole position in 1 min 14.846 sec, and Arnoux was alongside him on the front row of the grid with a time of 1 min 15.398 sec. With the Goodyear tyres superb on this circuit and the new Lucas-Ferrari mechanical ignition system performing perfectly, Alboreto went straight into the lead and quickly extended his advantage over Warwick (Renault) to six seconds. Arnoux was in third place, eight seconds behind Warwick. Alboreto led throughout the entire 70 laps of the race and at the finish was over 42 seconds ahead of the Renault driver, with Arnoux still in third place, having set a new lap record of 120.233 mph. At this race the McLarens had been plagued by problems in practice and the race and were never in serious contention. It seemed that Ferrari had got the equation right at last.

Michele Alboreto at the wheel of his 126C4 before practice for the 1984 Belgian Grand Prix.

The Belgian race was a magnificent success for Alboreto, for he took pole-position in practice and led throughout to win from Derek Warwick's Renault. Arnoux finished third.

This rather unattractive memorial to Gilles Villeneuve appeared at Zolder in 1984, two years after his death there in practice.

Michele Alboreto with his 126C4 at the 1984 Belgian Grand Prix at Zolder.

1984

At Zolder, Alboreto led throughout the race to score a fine victory.

René Arnoux in practice for the 1984 Monaco Grand Prix. The race was stopped early because of appalling wet weather conditions.

A fine cockpit shot of René Arnoux in wet practice at the French Grand Prix at Dijon in which he took fourth place.

As the season progressed the other turbocharged teams, especially McLaren, became increasingly dominant. Here in the Austrian Grand Prix Arnoux could manage no higher than seventh, while Alboreto took third place.

San Marino Grand Prix

At the San Marino race at Imola reality returned and the Ferraris reverted to mediocrity. Arnoux had set a quick time during Friday's damp practice, but was pushed down the grid to sixth place after a major engine blow-up. Alboreto was completely out of luck, for firstly his car ran out of fuel and when he took over his spare during the first session, he stopped because of injection failure. The result was that Arnoux was sixth fastest overall whilst poor Alboreto was back on the seventh row of the grid. At the end of the first lap Arnoux was in fourth place, but moved up to finish second behind Prost's winning McLaren, after Piquet's Brabham had been eliminated by turbocharger failure and Warwick had been slowed by gearbox problems on his Renault. Alboreto was eliminated early in the race; when he stopped to have a fluctuating turbocharger boost pressure investigated in the pits, the mechanics traced the trouble to a broken exhaust and the car had to be withdrawn.

French Grand Prix

That the Ferraris were on the slippery slope became only too evident at Dijon, where the team had four cars, the usual race cars for the two drivers,

The performance of the Ferraris at Monaco could best be described as mediocre. Here is Alboreto in practice in which he was third fastest and he finished seventh in the race.

but in addition both 071 and 072 as spares. On Alboreto's car there was a streamlined fairing round the gearbox and during practice this was also fitted to Arnoux' car. The two Ferraris were well off the pace and finished in practice back in tenth and 11th places. In the race Arnoux came through to finish fourth, gradually moving up the field as cars in front retired, but it had been an uninspired performance. Likewise, Alboreto drove a quiet and steady race until his engine expired on lap 34, never having risen above ninth place. Lauda won the race for McLaren

Sixth fastest in practice, Arnoux came through to finish second to Prost's McLaren in the San Marino Grand Prix at Imola.

from Tambay's Renault and with Mansell (Lotus) in third place.

Monaco Grand Prix

Once again Ferrari brought along four cars to Monaco, including a new car, 075, for Alboreto. And once again the team suffered a troubled practice. On the Thursday Alboreto set fastest time, but then hit the wall at Sainte Devote; his time was subsequently improved on and Arnoux was third fastest, slightly quicker than his team-mate.

On race day the weather was simply appalling, with thick low clouds and torrential rain. The organisers decided to spray the dry section of the circuit in the tunnel from a water tanker and this resulted in a delay in the start, but, in any event, a dry line had soon developed within a matter of laps. At the end of the first lap Arnoux and Alboreto were in third and fourth places, but Lauda with the McLaren passed them both. In these conditions Alboreto was thoroughly miserable, he spun and stalled his Ferrari,

In a wet, miserable race stopped at the end of 31 laps Arnoux, seen here on the climb from Sainte Devote, finished fourth behind Prost (McLaren), Senna (Toleman) and Bellof (Tyrrell).

was lapped by the leaders, and fell further and further behind. When race-leader Prost squeezed past Fabi's Brabham which had spun in the tunnel and was stationery in the middle of the track, Mansell was able to take advantage of the situation to grab the lead with his Lotus. However on lap 15 Mansell lost control on the slippery painted road markers on the climb from Sainte Devote and hit the guard rails. Although he attempted to get the car back to the pits, he was forced to abandon it at the Mirabeau.

Lauda spun on lap 24 and Ayrton Senna, pressing on with the Toleman, had moved up into second place behind race-leader Prost and was catching him rapidly. Clerk of the course, Jacky Ickx, who had been monitoring the race from television cameras placed around the circuit, brought the race to an end at the end of lap 31 and the eventual finishing order was Prost − Senna − Bellof (Tyrrell) − Arnoux, with Alboreto trailing in seventh place, a lap in arrears. It had been a thoroughly miserable parody of a race, in which few drivers had failed to make mistakes (Prost's driving had been faultless), but some of the younger drivers, particularly Senna and Bellof, had shown remarkable form in difficult conditions and had been able to exploit the advantages of their underpowered cars. For Ferrari it was a race best soon forgotten.

Canadian Grand Prix

For the Canadian race on the Circuit Gilles Villeneuve at Montreal in Quebec, Ferrari had 074 available as the spare car, whilst Arnoux drove 075 and there was a new car, 076, for Alboreto. Once again the 126C4s were plagued by handling problems and the adoption of narrow front track suspension did nothing to cure the problem. Qualifying was relatively trouble-free, at least in mechanical terms, although Arnoux had fuel pump bothers and an altercation between Alboreto and a group of Italian journalists led to him being thumped! In Canada Piquet (Brabham) was dominant, fastest in practice, and he led the race throughout, as well as setting fastest lap, not breaking the record but nearly equalling the existing record set by Pironi in 1982.

The Ferraris were back on the third row of the grid, with Arnoux slightly faster than Alboreto. In the race the Ferraris initially held third and fourth places but Alboreto was eliminated on lap 11 when his engine blew. With only four more laps completed Arnoux was in the pits for a change of tyres as his initial Goodyears were simply not up to the speed of the circuit and at the finish was back in fifth place, two laps behind the winner. With the consistency which had become only too familiar already in the season, the McLarens finished second and third.

United States (Detroit) Grand Prix

The American races continued a week later with the Detroit Grand Prix, held over a very tortuous and boring street circuit. The Ferrari drivers had the same cars as in Canada, but now equipped with the latest Marelli/Weber electronic fuel injection which Forghieri had now satisfied himself was likely to prove reliable. Whilst Alboreto had a trouble-free practice and finished fourth fastest, taking a place on the second row of the grid alongside Mansell's Lotus, Arnoux had a thoroughly miserable time in both practice and race. He seemed unable to get the hang of the circuit and after an engine failure during unofficial practice on the Saturday, sorted out in time for the final qualifying session, he spun at the exit of the chicane just before the pits and finally finished up with a place back on the eighth row of the grid, faster than Bellof's Tyrrell on the same row. From fourth place at the end of the first lap Alboreto steadily climbed up through the field until he took second place on lap 27, but in the closing stages of the race the Ferrari blew up, the result of a split intercooler . As for Arnoux, his race was soon over, for on lap 3 he spun into a wall and crawled round to the pits to retire.

United States (Dallas) Grand Prix

Right from the start of practice few drivers were happy with the Dallas circuit, for although it was a fast circuit and definitely more variable and

In the third successive race in North America, the Dallas Grand Prix, Arnoux drove a brilliant race. When his engine refused to fire on the parade lap, he was forced to start from the back of the grid and he fought his way through the field to finish second behind Rosberg (Williams).

interesting than Detroit, all were concerned about the bumpy surfaces, the lack of adequate run-off areas and the concrete walls that lined parts of the circuit. The handling of the Ferraris on the bumpy surfaces was particularly bad, but rather than try to sort out the handling problems, Forghieri concentrated mainly on adjustments to the injection and exhaust systems in an effort to improve performance. Despite his unhappiness with the circuit, Arnoux managed to achieve fourth fastest time in 1 min 37.785 sec, through sheer bravery, behind Mansell (Lotus), de Angelis (Lotus) and Warwick (Renault). Alboreto was much slower, back in ninth place, and over a second slower than his team-mate.

Immediately after the final parade lap before the start of the race, Arnoux' engine refused to fire and he was obliged to start from the back of the grid. As a result he completed the first lap of the race in 19th place, gradually clawing his way through the field and passing car after car, until he eventually came home second to Keke Rosberg's Williams and he and the Finn were the only two drivers to complete the full race distance. For Alboreto it was an unhappy race, for he never rose above seventh place and he was eliminated on lap 54, 13 laps from the finish when he hit a wall.

British Grand Prix

For the British race, Ferrari brought along 075 for Arnoux and 076 for Alboreto, with 073 and 074 as spares. The two race cars were now fitted with water radiators mounted longitudinally and installed beneath taller side-pods with top venting. Once again both cars were well off the pace, for both cars lacked grip on the Brands Hatch circuit. Alboreto was ninth fastest, despite an engine failure on the Friday and Arnoux was back in 13th place on the seventh row of the grid. Certainly the team could not look forward to the outcome of the race with any optimism.

During the opening laps of the race, both drivers were well down the field, but the red flag was shown at the end of lap 12 after Palmer's R.A.M. broke its steering and hit the tyre barriers on the outside at Clearways on lap 11. After the race had been restarted, the Ferraris still ran steadily but not particularly quickly and the only excitement for the Ferrari supporters were the two Ferrari drivers' attempts to pass Andrea de Cesaris with his Ligier, who was being more than a little obstructive. Lauda won the race for McLaren from Warwick (Renault), Senna (Toleman), de Angelis (Lotus) and with the Ferraris of Alboreto and Arnoux in fifth and sixth places, a lap in arrears. In the Constructors' Cup McLaren now led with 67.5 points, (half-points were awarded at Monaco) with Ferrari trailing second with 34.5 points.

German Grand Prix

At Hockenheim Ferrari again brought along four cars, and whilst two had the normal pull-rod rear spring damper units, two of the cars featured revised push-rod rear suspension together with reprofiled underbodies. These were 073, spare for Alboreto and 074, spare for Arnoux, whilst the race cars in original form were 072 for Alboreto and 075 for Arnoux. Neither of the drivers could make their minds up as to which was the preferable

The British Grand Prix at Brands Hatch proved another disappointment and the best that Ferrari could manage was fifth and sixth after slow times in practice. Here is Alboreto who finished fifth.

arrangement, but after Alboreto's race car developed electrical problems on the Saturday afternoon, he was forced to use the narrower suspension set-up. Neither Ferrari was on the pace, with Alboreto taking sixth place on the grid and Arnoux tenth.

De Angelis, who had been second fastest in practice to Prost's McLaren, led until lap 8 when the Renault engine broke and the race then devolved into a battle between Prost, the pace-setter, challenged by Lauda, and these two drivers took the first two places. Alboreto was eliminated by an engine misfire, whilst Arnoux who had won the race the previous year, finished sixth after a stop for new tyres. It could hardly have been a worse season for Ferrari.

Austrian Grand Prix

At the Österreichring the Ferraris had slipped even further. Here two of the cars seen at Brands Hatch with revised radiators now also featured a 5.1-in longer wheelbase and changed underwing. In Austria Alboreto had 076, while Arnoux had a new car, 077. The team had brought along 073 as spare for Alboreto and 074 as spare for Arnoux. Throughout practice Ferrari battled with different combinations of rear suspension, exhaust systems, undertrays and wheelbases, but the real problem was the lack of grip of the Goodyear tyres. Alboreto was

At the Österreichring Alboreto opted to drive through the race non-stop and his steady run resulted in third place, Ferrari's best performance for some races.

The McLaren with Porsche-designed and developed TAG engines dominated the year's racing. This is Niki Lauda who won in Austria.

12th fastest, with Arnoux back in 15th place. It was decided that Alboreto would drive 073 in the race. Lauda won for McLaren, with Piquet (Brabham) in second place, but despite his poor position on the grid, Alboreto made a good start and as the race progressed, gradually climbed up the field to finish third. Arnoux never in the running, made a pit stop for fresh Goodyear tyres and eventually finished seventh, a lap behind the leaders.

Dutch Grand Prix

Once again confusion reigned in the Ferrari camp, as the team struggled with four cars and different suspension arrangements. The spare cars were 073 for Alboreto and 077 for Arnoux, whilst 075 was to be Arnoux' race car and Alboreto had 076. Arnoux had opted for a 126C4/M car with longer wheelbase and new tubular rear suspension wishbones. Alboreto, whose car was fitted with similar wishbones, during the second practice session, eventually took ninth place on the grid, whilst Arnoux, who suffered turbo failure during Friday's practice and heat exchanger problems during Saturday's practice, took 15th place, back on the eighth row of the grid. Once again practice was dominated by Prost and Piquet. The McLarens of Prost and Lauda took the first two places in the race, whilst Piquet was an early retirement because of a loose oil union. As for the Ferraris there was not

much to be said, for Alboreto was eliminated on lap 8 by engine failure when holding ninth place and Arnoux was eliminated by electrical problems.

Italian Grand Prix

At Monza the Ferrari team produced two further modified C4/M2 cars with similar 'waisting' as featured on the McLarens and these cars were chassis numbers 072 and 074. These were intended to be raced, but in fact both drivers opted for their

Alboreto took a fine second place in the Italian Grand Prix at Monza. Note the tribute to Gilles Villeneuve painted on the road.

spare cars, Alboreto with 076 and Arnoux with 077. During practice on the Friday Alboreto, during a session with the odd rain shower, succeeded in achieving fourth fastest time, but by the end of Saturday's practice he had slipped back to 11th place on the grid with Arnoux three places behind and both Ferrari drivers were slower than the Benetton-sponsored Alfa Romeos of Patrese and Cheever. Arnoux was soon out of the race with gearbox problems, but it was to be Alboreto's lucky day. Although at the end of the first lap he was back in 11th place, as retirement followed retirement so Alboreto climbed up the field to take second place, the only other finisher on the same lap as the winner, and with Patrese's Alfa Romeo a lap in arrears in third place.

European Grand Prix

Just as in 1983 there had been an additional round of the World Championship under the title of European Grand Prix, held at Brands Hatch, so the German authorities were allowed to organise a European Grand Prix at the new and emasculated

Nürburgring. At this race both Alboreto and Arnoux drove the M2 Ferraris of McLaren configuration as seen in practice at Monza. Compared with earlier races in the season, both drivers were relatively happy with their cars, apart from understeering tendencies and they were also now much more on the pace, with Alboreto fifth fastest in 1 min 20.910 sec and with Arnoux sixth in 1 min 21.180 sec (compared with the fastest lap of Piquet in 1 min 18.871 sec).

On the first lap of the race, five cars were eliminated in three different accidents and by the end of the first lap Prost had pulled out a one-second lead over Tambay (Renault) followed by Piquet, Warwick (Renault) and with Alboreto and Arnoux holding fifth and sixth places. Alboreto challenged Warwick for fourth place, fighting hard to get past, with Lauda's McLaren breathing down his exhausts. Both Tambay and Warwick were eliminated by comparatively minor problems and this allowed Alboreto to move up into third place. On the very last lap, when Piquet was all set to finish second and gain six Championship points, the Brabham's engine started to cut out and Alboreto shot past. On the home straight the Ferrari began to cough and splutter and then it cut out completely. Alboretto coasted across to secure second place from Piquet by just a few feet.

An addition to the calendar in 1987 was the European Grand Prix run in October on the newly opened, emasculated Nürburgring. Again Alboreto was second behind the McLaren of Prost in this race. This is a practice photograph.

Arnoux, whose future with the Ferrari team had been slipping away, took fifth place at the Nürburgring.

Despite a spin earlier in the race, Lauda finished fourth and René Arnoux crossed the line to take fifth place for Ferrari. After a season that had been miserable for most of the time, Ferrari fortunes appeared to be on the up.

Portuguese Grand Prix

The last round in the Championship was the Portuguese race held on the Estoril circuit of 2.703 miles and with lap speeds of around 112-117 mph. Here the Ferrari drivers again opted for the M2 cars and Alboreto was reasonably satisfied with eighth place on the grid, splitting the Renaults of Tambay and Warwick. Poor Arnoux had his prospects of a good time ruined on the Saturday by a split turbocharger intercooler and he finished up with 17th fastest time and a place on the ninth row of the grid.

In the race Alboreto maintained contact with the front runners, and eventually finished fourth behind the McLarens of Prost and Lauda and Ayrton Senna (Toleman). Once again Arnoux was out of the picture back in ninth place.

In the World Championship, thanks to the combination of the speed and the reliability of the McLarens, Niki Lauda again won the World Championship with a total of 72 points, just half a

Arnoux' last race for Ferrari in 1984 ended on a low note. After problems in practice he drove a slow race to finish ninth, a lap in arrears, at Estoril.

point more than his team-mate Alain Prost. Third place in the Championship went to Elio de Angelis with 34 points, whilst Alboreto was fourth with 30.5 points. McLaren completely dominated the Constructors' Cup with 143.5 points, while Ferrari finished second, a very long way behind with 57.5 points. Perhaps the unluckiest combination of the season was Piquet with the Brabham, for Nelson Piquet could manage no better than fifth in the Championship and Brabham fourth in the Constructors' Cup; although they were undoubtedly the fastest combination racing in 1984, the BT53 Brabham suffered one of the worst reliability records.

5: *1985: A Year of Consistency*

Mauro Forghieri had been conspicuously absent from the late Grands Prix during the 1984 season, although Harvey Postlethwaite had attended certain races. The reason for Forghieri's absence was his concentration on a new design for 1985, an in-line 4-cylinder slant engine (in some ways aping the B.M.W.) but events were to prove that apart from compelling a high mounting for the turbocharger, it was not really up to scratch under power tests on the dynamometer. By this time Forghieri had been removed from the Formula 1 team and now was responsible for long-term projects. Under the control of Tomaini, development went ahead on slightly improved versions of the 1984 cars, which were typed the 156/85. In all nine new chassis were built, each differing slightly from each other, but the first batch of five differed rather more substantially from the second batch of four. The principal changes were low-mounted turbochargers instead of the former arrangement whereby the turbochargers were mounted in the vee of the engine, and the cars looked smooth and sleek, probably the best looking cars of the year. In constructing the new Ferraris, the team relied heavily on computer design support and modelling technology, utilising co-operation from Aermacchi, the Italian aeronautical concern and Gould Computers. However, as the season progressed, the other teams grew in power, in sheer horsepower terms, and Ferrari found themselves falling behind in the power race, and the dominant marque was to prove McLaren, although towards the end of the year both the B.M.W.-powered Brabham, the Honda-powered Williams and the Renault-powered Lotus had all overtaken Ferrari in terms of sheer bhp.

Brazilian Grand Prix

To the first race in the series Ferrari brought along as a spare 078, which was the car used for winter testing, whilst there was a new car, 079, for Alboreto and Arnoux drove another new car, 080. During practice on the Rio de Janeiro circuit Ferrari showed all the signs of impending dominance, for not only had Alboreto set fastest time during testing, but he was fastest in the untimed session on the Friday morning, third quickest in the afternoon and set fastest time in the final session on the Saturday afternoon. Perhaps unexpectedly second fastest was Keke Rosberg, with the Williams-Honda, and the Williams team had done a minimum of testing prior to the Brazilian race. Arnoux was in trouble throughout practice, his car was down on power on the Saturday and with his T-car he eventually set seventh fastest time.

Once again there was to be trouble at the start, for whilst Rosberg made a brilliant start as the light turned to green, Mansell with the second Williams, accelerated through from the third row of the grid

Ferrari started the 1985 season with good prospects, a combination of adequate power and competitive handling from the 156/85 cars, and in the Brazilian race at Rio de Janeiro Alboreto finished second. The race was won by Prost (McLaren).

and believed that he was ahead of Alboreto to take second place into the first corner, forcing the Ferrari to bounce off a kerb so that the left-hand front wheel hit the right-rear tyre of the Williams; the Williams rose into the air and spun across the grass and out of the race, whilst Alboreto continued in second place, heading Prost (McLaren) and the Lotus 97Ts of Senna and de Angelis. With only ten laps completed Rosberg was out with turbo failure and Alboreto moved into the lead, but Alboreto had his problems because of deranged front steering geometry as a result of the collision with Mansell. The Ferrari was able to accelerate away from Prost's McLaren along the straights, but the Frenchman with his McLaren hounded the Ferrari through the corners and when Alboreto missed a gear on lap 18, Prost shot into the lead.

Now Alboreto found Lauda with his McLaren on his tail. However Lauda was not able to hold third place for long, for on lap 23 he was forced to pull into the pits because of fuel metering problems. At the end of this 61-lap race, Alboreto finished second, a little over three seconds behind the McLaren. Arnoux had worked his way up through the field, but

on lap 27 de Cesaris (Ligier) rammed the back of the Ferrari and it was only after Arnoux had passed the pit lane entrance, that he realised that his left-hand rear tyre was deflating. After a full, slow lap, a new tyre was fitted and Arnoux rejoined the race, climbing back through the field to finish fourth, two laps in arrears.

It had been obvious for some while that relationships between Ferrari and René Arnoux had been deteriorating, especially after Arnoux' performances in the latter part of 1984, but after the French driver's stirring performance at Rio de Janeiro, it seemed that all would be well and that Arnoux had succeeded in rehabilitating himself in Enzo Ferrari's eyes. However this was not the case and there followed a meeting, at the invitation of Enzo Ferrari, on the Friday following the Brazilian race. After a heated discussion Arnoux left angrily and refused to turn up for a test session at the Fiorano test circuit the following day. There were further discussions and on the following Tuesday it was announced that Arnoux had requested to be released from his contract with the team, because of continuing problems with his leg muscles following surgery during the winter.

It was only too obvious that this was a subterfuge for the parties to go different ways and apparently Arnoux retained the major part of his fee for the 1985 season, said to be $US 1,000,000. The meeting with Arnoux had not been arranged without some thought as to his replacement, should things not go the way that Enzo Ferrari had intended, and immediately Stefan Johansson was released by Toleman to join Ferrari. In the meeting between Enzo Ferrari and Johansson, the *Commendatore* apparently asked but one important question, 'Are you a fighter?' to which Johansson replied in the affirmative, for, after all, had he not had to fight for everything? His place in the team was assured and within a matter of days he was practising in the drizzle at Estoril.

Portuguese Grand Prix

Having been the last race of the 1984 season, the 1985 race took place much earlier, on 21 April. Prior to the Portuguese race, in a test session at Fiorano, Ferrari had tried winglets mounted at the rear of the side pods, as fitted to the Lotus 79Ts, though rather larger, but these were abandoned because the aerodynamic advantages were nullified by the airflow to the turbocharger inlet duct being disturbed. At this race Alboreto drove 079, while Johansson had 080 and the team brought along

078 as a spare. Johansson had run well in testing at Fiorano and was very happy with the car, but was quickly disillusioned at Estoril where both Ferraris were giving their drivers a very bumpy ride. The young Swede found it difficult to accept Ferrari reassurances that this was a new phenomenon, not experienced in the first race in Brazil and one that would be easily cured. As for Alboreto, his main complaint was the Ferrari's lack of traction, but nevertheless he managed to take fifth position on the grid. Johansson was plagued by problems, gearbox trouble on the Friday and a rotor arm failure on the Saturday and he eventually made 11th fastest time in the T-car.

The vast strides that Gérard Ducarouge had made at Lotus with the 97Ts, was revealed by Senna's pole position and the fact that the two Lotus 97Ts of Senna and de Angelis dominated the first 42 laps of the race, run in cold and very wet conditions. Prost gradually closed up on de Angelis, with Alboreto close behind as the rain became heavier and heavier, Prost spun his McLaren and when de Angelis relaxed for a moment, Alboreto was able to slip through into second place on lap 43. He finished over a minute behind Senna, who had been the maestro in the wet, and he was the only driver not lapped by the Brazilian. Johansson finished eighth, after a spin, five laps in arrears.

The Portuguese race was won by Ayrton Senna with the Lotus 97T-Renault who battled all season with the McLarens, while Ferrari slipped further and further behind in the power race as the season progressed.

San Marino Grand Prix

At the Imola circuit Johansson drove 079 whilst there was a new car, 081, for Alboreto and once again the team had brought along 078 as the spare. There were a number of changes to the Ferraris, including the adoption of a tubular support inside the nose for the front wing and this was a direct result of the team's problems in changing the nose wing on Johansson's car at Estoril. During testing at Fiorano, the team had tried electronic control on the turbocharger wastegate, but it was not used at this race. Senna was again fastest in practice, but Alboreto was on the second row of the grid with a time of 1 min 27.871 sec, just over half a second slower than the pole-position time and Johansson, still feeling his way, was back on the eighth row of the grid with a time of 1 min 29.806 sec. It was a far from trouble-free practice for the Ferrari team, however, for although Alboreto was second fastest on the Friday, he was delayed by turbocharger problems on the Saturday and when he took out the T-car, rain prevented a fast time; so he had to rely on his time from Friday which was still good enough to give him his fourth place on the grid. Johansson had a frustrating time, because there were minor problems on the Friday, including the rear undertray working loose and most of his attempts at fast laps were baulked by traffic. Johansson's day, however, was still to come.

Again Senna and de Angelis set the pace in the opening laps, but Alboreto moved up into second place on lap 11 and remained there, despite pressure from Prost (McLaren) until lap 25 when the Ferrari slowed off and Alboreto pulled into the pits on the following lap where the mechanics worked on the electrics. Alboreto rejoined the race, all hopes of success lost, and set the fastest lap of the race in 1 min 30.961 sec (123.945 mph) before the electrical problems recurred and he was forced to retire. When Alboreto stopped, Johansson moved up into fifth place behind de Angelis and was gradually closing on the Italian Lotus driver. He moved up into fourth place on lap 37, ahead of Lauda's McLaren and then fought his way past de Angelis to take second place. Three laps before the finish Senna ran out of fuel in the Lotus-Renault and Johansson swept by into the lead, only to run out of fuel himself and allow Prost to go ahead again. The finishing order was Prost, de Angelis (Lotus), Boutsen (Arrows), Tambay (Renault) and Lauda (McLaren), but Prost's McLaren was found to be under the minimum weight limit at post-race scrutineering and was disqualified. So de Angelis and the others moved up a place and Johansson, despite running out of fuel, was classified sixth. All in all, a disappointing outing for Ferrari on home territory, but there was no doubting Johansson's potential.

Monaco Grand Prix

For the Monaco race Ferrari had made a number of changes to the car, in particular smaller turbochargers with a view to achieving greater power at lower revs, so important on this tortuous street circuit. Other changes included rear suspension with lower mounting points for the top wishbones, larger front brake ducts and the absence of a bypass between the intercooler and the wastegate. Alboreto had 081, whilst Johansson was entered with 079. There were two T-cars, 078 for Johansson and 080 for Alboreto. For the third race in succession, Ayrton Senna took pole position in 1 min 20.450 sec, with Alboreto third fastest in 1 min 20.563 sec. Despite a somewhat bumpy ride from his car, he had been

At Monaco Alboreto was second yet again, almost eight seconds behind Prost's winning McLaren. At this stage in the season Ferrari was still a team to be reckoned with.

Michele Alboreto joined the Ferrari
team from Tyrrell for 1984 and
remained with Ferrari until the end of
1988 – making him one of the longest-
serving Ferrari drivers – when he was
shown the door and rejoined Tyrrell,
who had provided his learning curve in
Formula 1.

The talents of young Swedish driver
Stefan Johansson were exploited by
Ferrari in 1985-6 and McLaren in
1987, without his true potential ever
being fulfilled. He is now with the
Onyx team.

The Ferrari pit at the 1985 Brazilian Grand Prix held on the Rio de Janeiro Autodrome.

Michele Alboreto in the French Grand Prix in which he retired early in the race because of turbocharger failure.

In the German Grand Prix in 1985 Alboreto scored a fine victory after the Williams and Lotus opposition ran into problems.

very much in the hunt for pole and it was a satisfactory grid position for Ferrari. Johansson was back on the eighth row of the grid, 15th place, in 1 min 22.635 sec, after a less than happy practice. On the Thursday he had tried his car with carbon-fibre brakes, and in this configuration it suddenly pulled to the left and shot down the escape road on the other side of the road, far from his intentions! During the Saturday practice session the Toleman of Teo Fabi moved across into him pushing his Ferrari into the barrier opposite the pits. In all the circumstances his position on the grid was not too appalling.

Whilst Senna shot off into the lead, followed by Mansell (Williams) and Alboreto driving hard and taking second place at the start of the second lap, Johansson was far less lucky. Berger (Arrows) made a slow start, Johansson pulled round him and was rammed by Tambay (Renault). Johansson completed

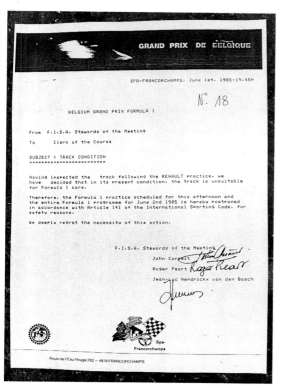

The formal notification of the postponement of the 1985 Belgian Grand Prix at Spa-Francorchamps because of the condition of the track.

the first lap, all four tyres were changed, but a lap later the car was retired because it was discovered that the accident had broken a damper rod on one of the rear shock absorbers of the Ferrari.

Throughout the early laps Alboreto kept the pressure on Senna and when Senna pulled into the pits on lap 13, Alboreto led the field, with Prost in second place with his McLaren. On lap 18 Alboreto slid at Sainte Devote, banging the Ferrari's nose against the barrier, keeping the engine running, and restarted behind Prost in second place. Alboreto pushed his way back into the lead on lap 23 when he passed the McLaren on the inside at Sainte Devote. However nine laps later Alboreto was slowed by the left hand rear tyre deflating and after a pit stop the Italian rejoined the race in fourth place with his Ferrari. He passed de Cesaris (Alfa Romeo) at the Mirabeau, and on lap 64 passed de Angelis (Lotus). Now light rain began to fall and at the fall of the flag at the end of lap 78 Alboreto was just under eight seconds behind the winning McLaren. Ferrari was now achieving consistency and the prospects for the team looked decidedly good.

Belgian Grand Prix

For the Belgian race on the Spa-Francorchamps circuit, Ferrari produced a new car 082 for Johansson, whilst Alboreto was at the wheel of 081. Alboreto's spare was 080. At Spa Ferrari introduced a new computer system whereby there was fuel consumption analysis read in the pits from a monitor; it was a promising system, but the team had doubts about its accuracy. Both cars had revised front suspension geometry and there was a new casting on the gearbox to accommodate the suspension pick-up points and a new rear wing support. The cars also were fitted with the electronic control on the turbocharger wastegate which had first been tried at Fiorano before the San Remo race. During practice for Spa, Alboreto was fastest with a lap in 1 min 56.046 sec (133.970 mph), all of eight seconds faster than the pole position time of Prost in 1983. However there were problems with the new track surface that was slippery and breaking up and despite efforts to repair the surface, the race was eventually postponed and re-scheduled for the 15 September.

Canadian Grand Prix

The teams now crossed the Atlantic for the races at Montreal and Detroit. At the Canadian race on the Gilles Villeneuve circuit, Alboreto again drove 081, whilst Johansson had 082. The spares were 080 for Johansson and 081 for Alboreto. On this circuit the team in practice tried the fuel consumption computer with a cockpit readout, but this was not used in the race. The cars ran with the electronic control on the turbocharger wastegate, and with no bypass between the heat exchanger and the turbocharger. In race trim the cars had very flat rear wings.

Once again the Lotus 97Ts were the fastest entries and de Angelis and Senna took the first two places on the grid, but the Ferraris were not far behind. Alboreto was third fastest in 1 min 25.127 sec (compared with de Angelis' time of 1 min 24.567 sec), a time set during the first practice session on the Friday. Alboreto's prospects of a better time on the Saturday were spoiled because of a disconnected oil line which resulted in the rear of his car catching fire. He was unable to improve on the time with the spare 156/85. Johansson had more

than his fair share of problems, spinning off into a wall during Friday's untimed session and breaking a steering arm; later he was plagued by clutch trouble and with his spare car that was jumping all over the road, he managed a time of 1 min 25.170 sec on the Saturday. At long last the Swedish driver seemed to have got on top of the idiosyncrasies of the Ferrari. Almost inevitably Lotus led the opening laps of the

In the two races on the Western side of the Atlantic Ferrari attained peak form. Here is the Canadian Grand Prix held on the Circuit Gilles Villeneuve at Montreal. Alboreto won the race, whilst new recruit to the Ferrari team Stefan Johansson finished second.

Alboreto and Johannson on the rostrum after their Montreal victory.

United States (Detroit) Grand Prix

Between the two North American races there were no changes to the Ferraris, apart from the substitution of new alternators because it had been realised by the team that those used at Montreal had only just lasted the race without failure. Once again on this street circuit the Ferraris were unhappy over the bumps, but even so Alboreto was third fastest, whilst Johansson, unhappy with lack of traction and understeer, was ninth fastest with a time of 1 min 44.921 sec, compared with pole-position man Senna's best lap in 1 min 42.051 sec. Senna led initially, but on lap 9 Rosberg took the lead with his Williams and all the while the Ferraris were keeping a watching brief. Rosberg went on to win the race for Williams, and the Ferraris of Johansson and Alboreto moved into second and third places, consolidating the form that they had shown in Montreal. During the closing laps of the race Johansson had pushed Rosberg hard, but his prospects of snatching the lead were ruined by rising turbocharger temperature and because a piece of paper blew into the right-front disc brake so that Johansson had to nurse the car for the last three laps.

Detroit proved a difficult race for the Ferrari team and the Scuderia's drivers proved no match for Rosberg (Williams). Here the mechanics work on the cars before the race.

race, with Senna ahead of Alboreto, until the Italian was able to swoop by on lap 16, and he succeeded in staying in front for the remainder of the 70 laps of this race. After a slow start, Johansson held fifth place, gradually moved up the field until lap 52 when, despite a slight misfire, he went ahead of de Angelis to take second place behind his team-mate. For the remainder of the race he pressured Alboreto and finished a mere 1.9 secs in arrears. It was the victory that Ferrari had been working for all season.

Here is Johansson who took second place at
Detroit, whilst Alboreto finished third to hold
his lead in the Drivers' Championship.

French Grand Prix

Before the French race Ferrari had tested at
Fiorano cars with revised monocoques, with
removable panels to facilitate access to the inboard
front spring/damper untis and with new front

suspension geometry. These cars were 081 and 083.
They were brought along to the Paul Ricard circuit,
but Alboreto found that he was faster with the older
spare car, 079, and with this he qualified third overall
behind Rosberg (Williams) and Senna (Lotus) and he
drove this car in the race. Johansson was right back
down the grid, because he was recovering from
chicken pox, not feeling very well and during the final
practice session, he missed fourth gear twice and so
ruined his chances of a good place. The Ferrari slide
in 1985 had started once again, for Alboreto was
eliminated on only lap 5 by turbocharger failure and
Johansson climbed up through the field to finish
fourth behind Piquet (Brabham), Rosberg (Williams)
and Prost (McLaren). Alboreto's retirement from the
race had been particularly dramatic, as the Ferrari
had blown up in a cloud of oil smoke which liberally
coated the track with oil and prevented any really fast
laps for some while.

British Grand Prix

For the Silverstone race there were few changes
to the Ferraris, but the position of the radiators had
been moved to allow a greater airflow to the
intercooler and during practice the team tried various
intercoolers and rear wings. After being plagued by
understeer at the Paul Ricard circuit, the cars now
seemed to have oversteer problems and it was also
clear that they were down on power compared with
some of their rivals. Alboretto took sixth place on the

Nelson Piquet, winner of the 1985 French Grand Prix at the Paul Ricard circuit at an average of
125.096 mph with his B.M.W.-powered Brabham BT54.

In the British race at Silverstone Johansson was rammed by Tambay (Renault) on the first lap. His team-mate however, finished second behind Prost's McLaren.

grid with a lap in 1 min 06.793 sec, with Johansson back on the sixth row with a time of 1 min 07.887 sec, compared with pole-position man Rosberg's time with his Williams of 1 min 05.591 sec.

At only the first corner of the race Tambay lost his Renault and slid sideways into the pack clouting Johansson's Ferrari. So far as Johansson was aware there was little damage to his car and he carried on, quite unaware that he was dropping oil all round the circuit and it was just as he reached the pits at the end of the first lap that the Ferrari's engine seized up. Alboreto started well down the field in seventh place, gradually moving up as retirement followed retirement, catching and passing Piquet (Brabham) on lap 28 while the Brazilian was trying to conserve his fuel because the fuel monitoring device had broken. There was so many retirements that the official flagging off the race became confused and stopped the race one lap early, but the winner Prost wisely carried on and finishing another lap to make sure that he at least had covered the official distance. Alboreto took second place, a lap in arrears, but his six points were at the expense of those who had retired rather than any other factor.

German Grand Prix

The German race at the *ersatz* Nürburgring was to prove the highlight of Ferrari's year. Alboreto drove 080 with 078 as a spare, whilst Johansson was entered with 079. There were few changes to the cars, but all three had the revised radiator positions seen at Silverstone and there were additional oil radiators placed horizontally at the rear of the engine covers. Remarkably, and showing the team's growing power, fastest in practice was Teo Fabi with his Toleman with a lap in 1 min 7.429 sec; whilst the next man on the grid Johansson with the Ferrari was over a second slower with a lap in 1 min 18.616 sec; the Swedish driver was at the peak of his form, very happy with his car at the Nürburgring. In contrast Alboreto seemed all at sea with his Ferrari and was half a second slower, back on the fourth row of the grid with a time of 1 min 19.14 sec.

When the green light came on for the start of the race, Johansson accelerated into the lead as Fabi made a slow start, but the Swedish driver was passed both by Senna and Rosberg; Alboreto tried to squeeze through on the inside of Johansson, the two Ferraris contacted and Alboreto's left front nose-fin punctured the right rear tyre on Johansson's car. At the end of that lap Johansson pulled into the pits for a wheel change and he rejoined the race in last position. In a lucky third place Alboreto held station, Senna passed Rosberg but Senna's Lotus retired on lap 27 with failure of a drive-shaft constant velocity joint. When Rosberg had an enormous slide in his Williams on lap 45, Alboreto took a chance, and

Driving a finely balanced race Michele Alboreto came through to win the 1985 German Grand Prix at the *ersatz* Nürburgring from Prost (McLaren) and Laffite (Ligier).

Alboreto's Ferrari before the start of the 1985 German Grand Prix.

forcing the Ferrari inside the Williams and bouncing over the inside kerb forced his way into the lead, whilst Prost moved up into second place. Alboreto was not challenged by Prost, for the McLaren driver had brake problems, he dropped behind after a spin and at the finish was over ten seconds behind the winning Ferrari. As the race progressed, so Johansson had been pulling up through the field, but ten laps from the finish he spun as a result of failing brakes and rejoined the race to finish ninth, a lap in arrears, whereas he should have at least finished in the points. With his consistent performances in earlier races and his win in Germany, Alboreto led the World Championship with 46 points to the 41 of Prost and the 26 of de Angelis, whilst Ferrari had a 19 point

lead (65 points to 46) over McLaren in the Constructors' Cup.

Austrian Grand Prix

As Ferrari struggled to increase the power of the 156/85 cars, so the team found themselves plagued by loss of engine reliability and during practice for the Austrian race the team suffered a total of four engine failures in the space of three days. In addition the cars were handling badly over the bumps once again, and the best that the drivers could manage, handicapped as they were, was 12th place on the grid by Johansson in 1 min 27.961 sec, with Alboreto slightly faster in 1 min 27.516 sec, but both were well off the pace and very slow compared with Prost's pole position in 1 min 25.490 sec.

At the start Fabi stalled his Toleman and in the ensuing mêlée Alboreto's Ferrari had its front suspension damaged. The race was stopped and started from scratch and this meant that Alboreto was able to rejoin with his spare car, 080. The Ferraris were never in contention for the lead, but had to settle for their own private struggle for fourth place, with Johansson time and time again trying to pass his Italian team-mate, but every time Alboreto shut the door and made it quite clear that he thought that he should stay in front, notwithstanding the fact that Johansson was clearly faster! Johansson was bemused by Alboreto's tactics, but eventually backed off and continued in station. Alboreto and Johansson finished third and fourth and in the World Championship Prost and Alboreto were level pegging with 50 points apiece.

Dutch Grand Prix

At the Dutch race Alboreto was entered with 080, whilst Johansson drove 079 and the team's spare was 078. During the first practice session Ferrari tried low-mounted additional rear wings to improve underbody air extraction and hopefully increase downforce and traction, but the idea was soon abandoned. At the Dutch circuit both Ferrari drivers were completely outclassed by the opposition, plagued as they were by the bad handling of the cars over the bumpy surface, unhappy with the unpredictable handling and suffered from wheelspin. Alboreto could manage no better than 16th fastest in 1 min 13.725 sec, with Johansson a row further back with a time of 1 min 13.768 sec.

In the race Johansson was an early retirement with engine failure, but mainly through persistency Alboreto came through to finish fourth behind the

So much of Ferrari was expected by the 'Tifosi' in the Italian Grand Prix at Monza, but the sole runner at the finish, Johansson, was back in fifth place.

McLarens of Lauda and Prost and Senna's third-place Lotus. So Alboreto dropped to second place in the World Championship with 53 points to the 56 of Prost, and McLaren with 70 points had closed within 5 points of Ferrari's lead in the Constructors' Cup. All was far from well at Maranello.

On the day after the race Renault the pioneer of turbocharged engines in Grand Prix racing announced their withdrawal from the sport at the end of the year. It was a sad decision, but it was also only too obvious that without major redevelopment the cars could no longer maintain any form of respectability against the newer turbocharged opposition and the poor state of Renault finances dictated a withdrawal from racing for diplomatic reasons if nothing else.

Italian Grand Prix

Ferrari was desperate to do well at Monza in front of the home crowd, and so there were three much modified cars. Extensive suspension modifications included new fixing points for the pull-rods front and rear and for the front shock absorbers; side radiators parallel to the monocoque; larger turbocharger intercoolers; narrow and shorter rear bodywork, possible because the turbocharger wastegate had been repositioned; and shorter rear bodywork, together with a lower engine cover. Johansson drove 083 in modified form whereas Alboreto's car, 085 was new; the team had as a spare, 084.

All these modifications did little good. The cars still lacked horsepower, still lacked traction and still suffered engine failures. Senna set fastest lap in practice in 1 min 25.084 sec, while Alboreto was back on the fourth row with a time of 1 min 26.468 sec and Johansson a row further back in 1 min 27.473 sec.

Early in the race Alboreto held fifth place, with Johansson eighth, and eventually Johansson took fifth place, a lap in arrears behind Prost (McLaren), Piquet (Brabham), Senna (Lotus) and Surer (Brabham). Alboreto was classified 13th, six laps in arrears after engine failure on lap 45, whilst holding fifth place. Not only was Alboreto now far behind in the World Championship with 53 points to the 65 of Prost, but Ferrari had slipped to second place in the Constructors' Cup with 77 points to the 79 of McLaren.

Belgian Grand Prix

Following the débâcle early in the year when it had been necessary for the Belgian Grand Prix to be postponed, the race was arranged again on 15 September. Ferrari brought along two of the modified cars as at Monza, 085 for Alboreto and 083 for Johansson, with 078 as the spare. A number of changes had been made, including new vertical front wings, ducts running from the turbocharger inlet to the rear shock absorbers and a new black box to monitor the engine performance during the race. At Spa the Ferraris were somewhat more competitive and Alboreto was fourth fastest in 1 min 56.021 sec, with Johansson on the next row in 1 min 56.585 sec; Prost took pole in 1 min 55.306 sec. Both Ferrari drivers were soon out of the race, Alboreto with a broken clutch and gearbox problems and Johansson when his Ferrari's engine seized and he spun off the circuit. The race was won by Ayrton Senna (Lotus), but Prost took third place and consolidated his lead over Alboreto in the World Championship.

European Grand Prix

To the European Grand Prix at Brands Hatch Ferrari brought along 085 for Alboreto and 086 for Johansson, whilst 083 was the spare. The cars had new triple-tier rear wings with revised profiles, the underbody was shorter, there were larger anti-roll bars at the rear and the engine lubrication system had been much modified. During practice Alboreto tried a revised KKK turbocharger on the Saturday, but this failed. The cars were still in trouble with lack of traction and Alboreto also suffered a broken turbo on

the spare car on the Friday. Both were well down the grid, Johansson 13th fastest in 1min 10.517 sec and Alboreto two places slower in 1 min 10.659 sec (compared with Senna's pole position time of 1 min 07.169 sec). When Alboreto suffered turbocharger failure with a fire of quite dramatic proportions, gone were his chances in the World Championship. Johansson had worked hard and had risen to fourth place, but was eliminated by alternator failure. The retirement of Alboreto had virtually ensured Prost's win in the Drivers Championship.

At the postponed Belgian Grand Prix at Spa-Francorchamps both Ferraris were eliminated early in the race and Alboreto slipped even further behind Prost in the World Championship. Here Alboreto is seen in the pits.

South African Grand Prix

For the South African race Ferrari were still struggling, trying smaller rear anti-roll bars and fitting new side-plates to the front wings to fill the space where former large brake ducts had been. Alboreto's car (083) had the older, long undertray and single rear wing, while Johansson's car (086) and the spare car (084) had short undertrays and an additional rear wing. Black gloom hung over the Ferrari team at Kyalami, for the cars still lacked traction, they still suffered from understeer into corners and oversteer and wheelspin on the exit from corners and compared with much of the opposition they were also slow in a straight line. On the straight to Marlboro corner the Ferraris were attaining around 195 mph, compared with the 210 mph of the Brabham BT54s. Both drivers were back on the eighth row of the grid, Alboreto in 1 min 05.268 sec and Johansson in 1 min 05.388 sec, faster only than the Tyrrells of Brundle and Streiff, the Minardi of Martini and the Osella of Rothengatter. On only the ninth lap Alboreto's turbocharger broke but Johansson drove a brave and forceful race, climbing up to seventh place by lap 11 and slowly moving up through the field to take fourth place, a lap in arrears. The race was dominated by the Williams-Hondas of Mansell and Rosberg which took the first two places.

Australian Grand Prix

The final and sixteenth round of the 1985 Championship was the newly inaugurated Australian Grand Prix on a 2.347-mile street circuit at Adelaide. Alboreto's 083 had a rear wing similar to the type used at the start of the season and a longer underbody, whilst both the spare car and Johansson's 086 had a shorter underbody and the triple rear wing. On the Saturday Johansson's car was fitted with a single rear wing. Alboreto's car was running on carbon-fibre brakes, whilst Johansson had cast-iron brakes. Alboreto ran better than he had at recent races and took fifth place on the grid in 1 min

By the Australian Grand Prix the Ferrari team was on the slippery slope. Here is Alboreto who was eliminated by gear-linkage problems. After having led the World Championship during the early part of the year, he eventually finished second, 20 points behind the winner, Alain Prost.

22.337 sec (compared with Senna's pole-position time of 1 min 19.843 sec), whilst Johansson was back on the eighth row with a time of 1 min 23.902 sec. Alboreto ran well in the race, holding third place, but falling back after an early pit stop for a new tyre and climbing back to fourth place until eliminated shortly before the finish, when holding third place, by a bolt falling out of the gear-change. Johansson drove a steady and unspectacular race to finish fifth, a lap in arrears.

After such a promising start to the season, it had been a hopelessly disappointing year for Ferrari and Alboreto; whilst still holding second place in the World Championship, the Italian had accumulated a total of 53 points compared to Prost's 73. It was much the same story in the Constructors' Cup which McLaren won with 90 points from the 82 of Ferrari. Despite having better resources than any other Grand Prix team and better finance than most, Ferrari was providing miserably unsuccessful in putting its act together and achieving the domination that should be expected of such a powerful team.

6: *1986: The Decline Continues*

Both Alboreto and Johansson stayed with Ferrari for 1986 and the team raced the F1/86, a developed version of the 1985 car with substantial improvements so far as roadholding and traction were concerned, but deficient in aerodynamics compared with certain of the other teams and gradually declining in the power race, with a maximum output of around 850 bhp at 11,500 rpm, a good 50 bhp down on the B.M.W.-powered cars. In 1986 Ferrari adopted Garrett turbochargers initially for the race only and not for qualifying. Compared with the 1985 cars, the new Ferraris were much lower, with the roll-over bar enclosed in the rear bodywork and the carbon-fibre chassis built on the same lines as Williams, with separate floor section and main monocoque, the front dampers mounted horizontally, a new, longer-profile under-body and with the rear wing centrally mounted on two carbon-fibre plates. Unfortunately the Ferraris were to prove uncompetitive throughout most of the year and few satisfactory performances were achieved.

Brazilian Grand Prix

For the race at Rio de Janeiro Ferrari brought along two of the new 1986 cars, 087 for Johansson, 088 for Alboreto, together with one of the 1985 cars, 085 fitted with the front suspension and front uprights from the F1/86 model. No one was expecting much of the Ferraris after their poor performances in the latter part of 1985, but the cars showed considerable speed in a straight line and Alboreto managed sixth place on the grid in 1 min 27.485 sec with the 1985 car, while Johansson was two places slower in 1 min 27.711 sec (compared with pole-position Senna with the Lotus in 1 min 25.501 sec). Although both cars ran towards the front of the field, some distance behind the leaders, both retired, Johansson with brake trouble which resulted in him becoming bogged in a sandy run-off area, whilst Alboreto was eliminated by a broken fuel pump drive. The race was won by Nelson Piquet (Williams-Honda).

Spanish Grand Prix

After an interval of five years the Spanish Grand Prix was resurrected on a new circuit at Jerez, right in the Spanish sherry-producing country, in an area that had a poor spectator catchment. It was, however, a bumpy circuit and so the Ferrari drivers had an even rougher ride than usual. Again Alboreto drove 088, and Johansson had 087, with a new car, 089 as spare. There were few changes to the cars, although there were new front anti-roll bars, stronger fixing plates for the disc brakes, modified turbochargers and for the race both cars were fitted with double rear wings. After a petrol fire in the engine bay

Johansson took 11th place on the grid, whilst Alboreto who suffered two broken drive-shafts on the Friday during experiments with a new differential was 13th. In the race both cars ran rather uninspiredly behind the first half dozen runners. At the end of lap 11 Johansson was about to overtake Laffite's Ligier when the brakes failed and the Ferrari went straight into the tyre-lined guard rail. The cause of the problem was a brake bleed nipple that had worked loose and allowed the brake fluid to escape. The Ferrari was wrecked and Johansson suffered a bad shaking and bruising. Eighteen laps later Alboreto was out of the race because a wheel bearing had started to break up. The Spanish Grand Prix was won by Ayrton Senna (Lotus-Renault) from Mansell (Williams-Honda).

San Marino Grand Prix

For the Imola race Ferrari produced a new car for Johansson, 090, whilst Alboreto retained 088 and the team brought along 089 as a spare. Prior to this race Ferrari had carried out extensive tests at Imola, but changes to the cars were of a detailed nature only. The Ferraris showed slightly better form and Alboreto was fifth fastest in practice in 1 min

The 1986 installation of the Ferrari V-6 turbocharged engine.

26.263 sec, compared with pole-position man Senna's best lap of 1 min 25.050 sec and Alboreto commented that the handling of the car was much improved. Johansson, who suffered brake trouble during qualifying and a slow puncture, was two places lower on the grid in 1 min 27.009 sec. In the race the Ferraris ran well and Alboreto moved up to fourth place on lap 12, while Johansson, still suffering brake

The 1986 season was a three-cornered battle between Lotus, Williams and McLaren with no role for Ferrari. Here is Johansson in the Spanish race at Jerez where he lost his brakes and crashed into the guard-rail on lap 12.

troubles and having to pump the brakes, was in ninth place. On lap 57 Alboreto rolled into the pits to retire with turbocharger failure; as the result of attempts to run on a leaner fuel mixture to improve economy, the tips of the turbine wheel had broken. Alboreto was classified tenth. Johansson took fourth place, a lap in arrears, behind Prost (McLaren), Piquet (Williams) and Berger (Benetton).

Monaco Grand Prix

At the Monaco race the drivers had the same cars as at Imola and again 089 was the spare. The team also brought along 092 which had not been completed. In accordance with what had become usual Ferrari practice, the engines were specially set up for Monaco to give improved torque at low revs

and were fitted with smaller turbochargers; there was a throttle-linked, mechanically operated butterfly assembly, which was intended to improve engine response. Both cars ran with a double rear wing. There was an important change to the braking. In 1986 Ferrari had fitted calipers of their own make, but following Johansson's bad crash at Jerez and the brake troubles he had suffered at Imola, Ferrari had reverted by Monaco to calipers of Brembo manufacture.

The Ferraris were still uncompetitive as practice soon revealed, but Alboreto, in the final session, turned in one really outstanding lap, the Ferrari dancing over Monaco's bumps and the Italian controlling its notorious understeer by large bursts of throttle, and finishing the lap with four wrecked wheels and a place on the second row of the grid in 1 min 23.904 sec. Poor Johansson was back on the

Stefan Johansson at Monaco in 1986. He finished tenth, three laps in arrears, after a race of problems.

At Monaco in 1986 Michele Alboreto leads Keke Rosberg (McLaren MP4/2C). Alboreto was holding fourth place when he retired with turbocharger failure on lap 39.

Alboreto again, in the British race at Brands Hatch, where he again retired with turbocharger failure when holding fifth place.

The shunt at the start of the 1986 German Grand Prix. Alliot (Lola, No. 26) accelerated into Joahansson's Ferrari (No. 28) which in turn was shoved into the Benetton of Fabi. Johansson crawled round to the pits for a new nose-cone to be fitted and was classified 11th (but not running because of a broken rear wing).

Left: Johansson with his F/186 at the 1986 Portuguese Grand Prix.

Below: In the Portuguese Grand Prix at Estoril, Johannson finished sixth, a lap in arrears.

Johansson's final drive for Ferrari was in the 1986 Australian Grand Prix at Adelaide where he finished third. Here he is seen leading Ayrton Senna's Lotus 98T.

At the end of 1986 Johansson was replaced in the Ferrari team by Gerhard Berger who had driven superbly for Benetton. Berger remains a member of Ferrari in 1989.

eighth row with a time of 1 min 25.907 sec. At the end of the final practice Johansson — through no fault of his own — was involved in a particularly nasty accident. A rear wheel of the Ferrari struck Renault technician Jean Sage as Johansson drove into the pits, the Frenchman was thrown in the air and lucky to escape with a broken shoulder and concussion.

Alboreto could not match his qualifying performance in the race and after holding fourth place, he retired on lap 39 with turbocharger failure. Despite appalling handling and a broken gear-lever (with so many gear changes per lap, this is the worst circuit for such a misfortune to occur), the Swedish driver struggled on to finish tenth, three laps in arrears. The McLarens of Prost and Rosberg took the first two places.

Belgian Grand Prix

At this race Alboreto drove 089, whilst Johansson retained 090 and there was a new spare, 091. Garrett turbochargers were fitted to the two race cars on the Thursday, whilst the T-car still retained the KKK turbochargers. However by the Friday all three cars were back on KKK turbochargers. In an effort to improve the handling, the rear suspension had been modified with new top mounting points for the push-rods and new fabricated uprights. Practice soon revealed that these changes had done nothing to solve the understeer and lack of traction. Whilst Alboreto was ninth fastest in 1 min 56.242 sec and Johansson 11th fastest in 1 min 56.496 sec (compared with Piquet's 1 min 54.331 sec to take pole with the Williams), there was a smaller consolation that through the time-trap Alboreto was fastest in the last session with a speed of 199.667 mph. The sensation of practice however was Berger with the Benetton who was fastest during the first day's practice and eventually took second place on the grid.

In the race the Ferraris were to achieve a reasonable result, mainly because of a first lap accident that put several of the entries out of contention. Whilst Piquet accelerated away from the start into the distance, Prost followed him through,

At Monaco Alboreto leads Keke Rosberg (McLaren). The Italian retired because of turbocharger failure, but Rosberg finished second.

Berger, slow away, moved to the right whilst Senna went round the outside of the Austrian with his Lotus. As the cars braked for La Source hairpin, they were three abreast. Prost's and Berger's wheels locked and the McLaren was catapulted on to the kerbing; whilst Rosberg took the escape road with his Williams, Fabi's Benetton stopped because of the chaos and Tambay's Lola wrecked its left front suspension on the right rear of Fabi's car. Tambay was out of the race but Berger and Prost managed to keep going and complete a lap before coming into the pits for repairs. The race settled down to Piquet leading Senna (but Mansell took second place on lap 3), with Johansson now fourth in the ill-handling Ferrari, and protected by Johnny Dumfries in fifth place with the Lotus, effectively blocking the progress of Jones (Lola) Laffite (Ligier) and Alboreto. When Mansell spun on lap 5 Johansson moved up into third place, but Mansell recovered third spot as they braked for Les Combes on lap 15. As the result of pit stops for new tyres, Johansson led briefly, on laps 22 and 23, and rejoined after his own pit stop in fourth place behind

The Belgian Grand Prix at Spa-Francorchamps, won by Mansell (Williams) from Senna (Lotus), proved one of Ferrari's better races in 1986. Johansson (above) finished third.

Alboreto. Despite 'slow' signals from the Ferrari pit, Johansson and Alboreto battled for third place, with Alboreto who had decided to run on the harder compound B tyres unable to hold off the Swedish driver who slipped by into third place on lap 38. When the race finished at the end of lap 43, Piquet still led from Senna, wth the Ferraris of Johansson and Alboreto in third and fourth places.

Canadian Grand Prix

For the Canadian race a number of changes were made to the cars, including a modified underbody which featured separate exhaust pipes (seen on Renaults in 1983). In addition there were new Speedline wheels with one-piece rims. Alboreto drove 092, the car brought to Monaco in an unfinished state, whilst Johansson drove 091. The team spare was 090. During qualifying Ferrari suffered a total of five turbocharger failures, which resulted in Garrett having to bring spare turbochargers to the circuit. The problem, it seems, was caused by a build up in exhaust back pressure causing failure of the turbine thrust bearings and quite probably the result of the revised underbody. In any event Ferrari reverted to the original underbody configuration for the final qualifying session on the

Saturday. With all these problems, coupled with the fact that the cars were still handling badly and bouncing on the bumps, Alboreto could manage no higher than 11th place on the grid with a time of 1 min 27.495 sec, whilst Johansson was back in 18th place in 1 min 28.881 sec (pole postion went to Mansell with the Williams in 1 min 24.118 sec).

The Ferraris were never in contention in the race, but Johansson and Alboreto came through to hold seventh and eighth places. Johansson's race came to an end on lap 31. At the Esses just past the pits, Johansson came across Dumfries (Lotus) on the racing line still building up speed after a pit stop. Johansson moved across to overtake on the right, but unfortunately Dumfries moved that way so as to give room for Johansson on the left. The Ferrari rammed the Lotus, both cars were put out of the race, and Alboreto spun to avoid a collision. As he spun Alboreto struck his leg against the underside of the Ferrari's steering rack, bruising himself quite badly and, badly shaken by this close shave and, later in the race, losing a couple of gears, he toured round to finish eighth, a lap in arrears. The race was won by Nigel Mansell (Williams-Honda) with Alain Prost (McLaren) in second place.

United States (Detroit) Grand Prix

For this race Alboreto once again had 092, whilst Johansson drove 086. This had originally been built to the 1985 156/85 specification but had been broken up following discovery of a structural problem. It had now been completed and was used to replace 091 which had been badly damaged in Johansson's Montreal crash and was not raced again. The spare was again 090. Changes to the cars at this race included a new turbocharger lubrication system and a previously untested twin brake system; additional pipes ran to the calipers from twin pumps and a further vent in the nose was needed. Both cars had the machined upper rear wishbones first seen in Canada, but the older wishbones were retained on the T-car. It seemed that Ferrari would never be able to resolve their understeer problems and the severe bouncing over bumps and Detroit was a particularly bumpy circuit. By sheer press-on bravado and using the throttle to convert the inherent understeer of the Ferrari into oversteer, Johansson managed to take fifth place on the grid with a time of 1 min 40.312 sec. The bruising that Alboreto had suffered in Canada whilst avoiding Johansson's crash caused him serious problems on Detroit's bumps and the best he

could manage in practice was 11th fastest in 1 min 41.606 sec (compared with Senna's pole in 1 min 38.301 sec). During Sunday morning's warm-up Johansson was seen out with Mansell's spare helmet, because when Johansson had gone to the Ferrari pits, his own helmet had been missing. In the race Johansson was eliminated by electrical problems, but Alboreto drove steadily to finish fourth. The sensation of the race was Ayrton Senna with the Lotus, who led until a tyre punctured and then fought his way back through the field to win from Laffite's Ligier.

French Grand Prix

Following Elio de Angelis' fatal accident during testing with his Brabham earlier in the year, planned changes to the Paul Ricard circuit were rushed through in time for the 1986 race; a link road, between the start and finish straight and the Mistral straight, reduced the length of the circuit from 3.6 to 2.36 miles and much improved circuit safety. Both race Ferraris, 092 for Alboreto and a new car 093 for Johansson, featured modified front suspension with the wishbones angled forwards so that the

Plagued by understeer, Stefan Johansson managed to take fifth place on the grid at Detroit, but was eliminated by electrical trouble on lap 41 when holding sixth place.

4, 5, 6, Juillet 86
circuit PAUL RICARD

72ᵉ GRAND PRIX DE FRANCE F.1

wheelbase was increased by 45 mm. The slightly longer wheelbase appeared to have reduced the understeer and both drivers were happier with their cars, although both were still well off the pace. Alboreto was sixth fastest, despite tangling with Prost on the Saturday afternoon; when Prost lifted off sharply when he saw an oil flag, Alboreto's right rear wheel hit the left front of the McLaren and the Ferrari was launched over the kerb reappearing on the track beyond the apex of the corner. Johansson could manage only tenth fastest in 1 min 07.874 sec (compared with Senna's pole in 1 min 06.526 sec).

At the start Alboreto stalled his engine and eventually finished eighth. Johansson was an early victim of turbocharger failure, retiring on lap 6. The race was won by Nigel Mansell with the Williams-Honda.

British Grand Prix

At Brands Hatch the Ferraris were 092 for Alboreto and 093 for Johansson, whilst the T-car was 089, all fitted with the new front suspension as seen in France. The cars had wider rear wings with larger side-plates. There were also differences between the two team cars for Alboreto's Ferrari had a skirt around the nose-cone, a double rear wing and stiffer suspension. At this race Ferrari used the KKK turbochargers for qualifying, but the Garretts were installed for the race. Qualifying proved a shambles for the Ferrari team. On the Friday both drivers were a good three seconds off the pace dictated by the Williams-Honda team and Ferrari were still struggling with understeer and trying to find traction. On the Saturday Johansson's engine blew, causing him to spin at Druids, whilst Alboreto suffered a turbocharger fire. Alboreto pulled off near the pits and returned on foot with a view to taking out the T-car, but Johansson was already at the wheel. Johansson had to give way to Alboreto and was forced to rely on his Friday time of 1 min 11.500 sec, only 18th fastest, whilst Alboreto was able to turn in 1 min 10.338 sec for 12th place on the grid. Although the cars had good straight-line speed, they were pathetically slow compared with the faster opposition and Piquet with his Williams took pole position in 1 min 06.961 sec. On the first lap of the race there was a multi-car accident at Paddock Hill

The French Grand Prix in 1986 was not a happy race for Alboreto, for in practice he collided with Prost, he stalled on the grid and finished the race well down the field in eighth place.

The British Grand Prix at Brands Hatch was another unhappy race for Ferrari and both Alboreto (seen here at Paddock Bend) and Johansson retired.

bend when Boutsen locked up the brakes on his Arrows. Johansson swerved to the right and Laffite was forced to go to his right and rammed the barrier head on, suffering bad leg and pelvis injuries. Seven other cars were involved in the mêlée and the race was immediately stopped. Johansson's miserable weekend ended after 20 laps of the restarted race when he came into the pits with his Ferrari pouring out clouds of smoke. It seemed that a stone had gone through the radiator, but as Stefan commented to journalists, 'there was another problem somewhere from the start of the race, the car just had no power at all.' Alboreto worked his way up to fifth place, only to retire because of turbocharger failure. The race was again won by Nigel Mansell (Williams-Honda) who led home team-mate Nelson Piquet.

German Grand Prix

For the German race there were a substantial number of changes to the T-car, which was 090. This had a new shorter wheelbase, by 125 mm by removal of the bell-housing. Because the oil tank had previously been inside the bell-housing, it now had to be repositioned above the gearbox and this meant that the rear suspension shock absorber mountings had to be repositioned. In this form the car had been tested at the Paul Ricard circuit. Whilst there were new rear wishbones and uprights, the new rear suspension layout was similar to a system tested at the Nürburgring in 1984. Other changes were a new rear wing with side-plates similar to those of the McLarens, and a new underbody with a single exhaust pipe. All three cars, including the race cars, 092 and 093 for Johansson, had the suspension with angled wishbones first seen at the Paul Ricard circuit.

Ferrari decided to use the Garrett turbochargers in qualifying, but it was to be a whole saga of blow-ups. Stefan Johansson reported, 'I had two engines blow on Friday morning, so I missed a lot of the timed session. I did one run and then had a turbo failure on the second and had to walk in. Another engine went this morning and I had to walk in again. It's getting difficult to keep track . . .' As for Alboreto, he reported one blown turbo, on the Saturday morning, but also had problems with the gear selectors. Both drivers were happy with the straight-line speed of the cars, but commented that almost everyone was quicker than the Ferraris through the corners. Alboreto was tenth fastest in 1 min 44.308 sec and Johansson recorded 1 min 44.346 sec

(compared with Rosberg's pole-position time of 1 min 42.013 sec).

The Hockenheim race was yet another marred by a start line accident. Arnoux (Ligier) found himself being out-accelerated by Fabi (Benetton), moved over to the right to force Fabi to back off, which caused Johansson to veer left to miss the back of the Benetton and into the path of Alliot (Ligier); as the two cars collided, Johansson's Ferrari was spun round into Fabi. Johansson's car lost its nose-wing and the Ligier had a puncture in the right front tyre. Johansson, whose frustrations at Ferrari were becoming almost unbearable, went straight up to Alliot after the race and hit him. Alboreto brought his Ferrari through to ninth place, but retired at the Ostkurve with a broken differential. Johansson was not running at the finish because of a broken rear wing, but was classified 11th.

Hungarian Grand Prix

Next on the calendar was the new Hungarian Grand Prix, held on a 2.49-mile circuit, set in a valley about 12 miles north-east of Budapest. Here further modifications had been carried out to the Ferraris and the race cars (090 for Johansson and 092 for Alboreto) had rear wings with longer side-plates and the bodywork had additional ducts for the turbochargers. The T-car, 088, had the rear wing

In the first Hungarian Grand Prix on the Hungaroring Stefan Johansson drove a good race to finish fourth, a lap in arrears behind Piquet (Williams), Senna (Lotus) and Mansell (Williams).

The first-lap shunt at the German Grand Prix. This photograph follows in sequence that shown on page 98. Here Johansson strikes Fabi's Benetton.

tried at Hockenheim and the twin brake system that had been seen at Detroit.

By a combination of wing and bravery Johansson succeeded in qualifying seventh in 1 min 31.850 sec, while Alboreto, whose car shed a front wheel during practice, was well down the grid in 15th place in 1 min 33.063 sec (compared with Senna's pole of 1 min 29.450 sec).

After two stops for tyre changes Johansson finished fourth, a lap in arrears, but Alboreto was eliminated in a collision with Warwick's Brabham; the B.M.W. engine of the Brabham had missed and Alboreto had slammed into the rear of the car, forcing both of them into retirement. The race was won by Piquet (Williams-Honda) from Senna (Lotus-Renault) and Mansell (Williams-Honda).

Austrian Grand Prix

There were few changes to the Ferraris at the Österreichring, apart from modifications to the nose-sections, with the nose-cone, wings and mounting tube in one piece to permit easy removal, because it had not been possible to repair the damaged nose of Alboreto's car at the Hungaroring, and there were detailed changes to the rear wings. On the Friday, Johansson spun off at the Hella-Licht chicane, and crossed the grass until the car came to rest against a steel pole supporting an advertisement hoarding. The

pole punched through the base of the monocoque and into the bulkhead behind the seat, causing Johansson considerable pain all weekend. He switched to the spare car, 089, but had problems with the engine cutting out. On the Saturday he crashed again; finding far more travel than he expected in the brake pedal, he pumped the pedal, locked the brakes at the Rindtkurve, the back end came round and clouted the barrier, damaging the right rear suspension and the gearbox. Later he qualified 14th in 1 min 26.646 sec, but was in so much pain that he was having to raise himself off the seat as he came to the bad bumps. In contrast, Alboreto's practice was untroubled and he took ninth place in 1 min 25.661 sec. As an indication of the growing power of the Benettons, their two drivers, Fabi and Berger, took first two places on the grid with times of 1 min 23.549 sec and 1 min 23.743 sec. The race was very much one of attrition, Fabi retired his Benetton when he had just taken the lead from team-mate Berger, Berger spent a long time in the pits and lost all chances of success because of a flat battery, both Mansell and Piquet retired their Williams-Hondas, Rosberg's McLaren was eliminated by electrical trouble, and so Prost won the race for McLaren, with Alboreto second, a lap in arrears, and Johansson, who had been in terrible pain throughout the race, third, two laps in arrears, having lost time in the pits while the front wing was sorted out. The Ferrari drivers were well pleased to finish up in the results, but as Alboreto pointed out afterwards, Prost was a lap and a half ahead at the finish.

Alboreto on his way to second place in the Austrian Grand Prix, albeit a lap behind Prost's winning McLaren.

Italian Grand Prix

More changes were made to the Ferraris at Monza where revised turbochargers and intercoolers were fitted. The race cars, 092 and 093, also featured Marzocchi shock absorbers which had separate gas cylinders. The spare car was 088. Alboreto missed the first day's practice and wide-ranging rumours spread as to his absence. It seems that the cause was a minor motor-cycle accident in which he had dislocated a shoulder. During Friday's practice Johansson was able to use Alboreto's special qualifying engine and he reckoned that it had far more poke than any Ferrari that he had driven previously. Alboreto was ninth fastest in 1 min 25.549 sec, with Johansson three places lower on the grid in 1 min 26.422 sec. Again the Benettons were amongst the fastest cars and Fabi took pole position with his Benetton in 1 min 24.078 sec. Whilst Berger set a burning pace in the opening laps, destined to take its toll both of his tyres and his fuel consumption, Mansell and Piquet held second and third places with Alboreto fourth. On lap 17 Alboreto spun at a bump coming out of the first chicane, striking the right-hand barrier and bending

Johansson turned in another good performance at Monza to finish third in the Italian Grand Prix behind the Williams-Hondas of Piquet and Mansell.

two wheels. After a pit stop he resumed in 11th place, climbing up to hold fifth behind Johansson, but his engine blew on lap 34. Piquet and Mansell took the first two places with their Williams-Hondas and Johansson finished third, ahead of Rosberg (McLaren) and Berger (Benetton) who had been forced to ease his pace to conserve fuel and had then been slowed by an engine misfire.

Portuguese Grand Prix

At the Estoril race there were only detail changes from the form in which the cars had been seen at Monza, but a new car, 094, was brought along as a spare. Johansson had been told that his services would not be required at Maranello in 1987, and whilst this soon became common knowledge, Johansson was very restrained in keeping off the subject! For once he had a trouble-free practice, qualifying eighth in 1 min 19.332 sec, whilst Alboreto was three rows further back with a time of 1 min 20.019 sec. During Saturday afternoon's qualifying Alboreto's right aerofoil began to disintegrate, the front right wheel began to lock up and when he reached the start/finish area the whole nose and wing assembly fell apart, puncturing a front tyre.

Both Ferraris ran steadily, but not spectacularly in the race, and Johansson began to close up on Berger's Benetton in fifth place. On lap 45 Johansson passed the Benetton at the right-hand corner following the pits; Berger tried desperately to get his place back, scrabbling round on the inside with two wheels up the kerb, but slamming into the Ferrari so that both cars spun off into the sandy run-off area. Johansson was able to keep his engine running and managed to rejoin the race, although the cooling duct to the right-hand turbocharger was damaged. Berger stalled the Benetton and was unable to restart. Johansson now dropped back to sixth place behind Alboreto and the two cars finished fifth and sixth behind Mansell (Williams), Prost (McLaren), Piquet (Williams) and Senna (Lotus).

Mexican Grand Prix

Sixteen years had elapsed since Mexico had last hosted a round in the World Championship, and the circuit now used was the old Autodromo Ricardo Rodriguez, completely updated and known as the Autodromo Hermanos Rodriguez. Because of the high altitude at which the race was held (7500 ft above sea level) and the effect that this had in reducing throttle response on turbocharged Grand Prix cars, Ferrari tried various permutations of Garrett turbos on the three cars, which were the same as at Estoril. No circuit throughout the year had exposed the shortcomings of the Ferrari chassis so much as Mexico and the Ferraris bumped and bounced their way round the circuit, between engine and turbo failures, for Alboreto to take 12th place on the grid in 1 min 19.388 secs with Johansson on the row behind in 1 min 19.769 sec (compared with Senna's pole of 1 min 16.990 sec). Alboreto was an early retirement on lap 11 with a blown turbo when going well in fifth place, but on his retirement Johansson moved up to fifth and, running strongly, holding fourth place until lap 65 when his turbo blew. Although not running at the finish he was classified 12th, four laps in arrears. The race proved a magnificent triumph for Gerhard Berger who scored his first Grand Prix win after so many disappointments earlier in the year, with Prost (McLaren) second and Senna (Lotus) third.

Australian Grand Prix

At Adelaide both Ferrari drivers crashed in practice. On the Friday Alboreto lost control and hit a wall head-on, writing off the monocoque and the team built up for him 089 which had been brought along as a spare. During the Friday afternoon official qualifying Johansson lost control and spun on a wet section of track, hit a concrete wall sideways and the left front wheel was pushed back into the monocoque. Luckily, Johansson's only injuries were a bruised ankle, shin and knee, but the car was a total write-off and he had to race what was the original spare, 094. After all his problems Alboreto qualified ninth in 1 min 21.709 sec, with Johansson a row back in 1 min 22.050 sec. Nigel Mansell with his Williams took pole in 1 min 18.403 sec.

Alboreto's race was soon over, for he was struck up the rear at the start and was put out of the race immediately. Johansson turned in a stirring race to finish third, a lap in arrears. This was the famous race which Prost won for McLaren, after the left rear tyre on Nigel Mansell's Williams-Honda blew on lap 64, ruining his prospects of winning the World Championship. As it was Prost took the Championship with 72 points to the 70 of Mansell, while Johansson was fifth with 23 points and Alboreto eighth equal (with Laffite and Arnoux) with 14 points. In the Constructors' Cup Ferrari had slipped to 37 points compared to the 141 of winners Williams-Honda, 96 of McLaren-TAG and the 60 of Lotus-Renault. Ferrari had sunk to a nadir from which the team was slow to recover and it is only now in 1989 that real recovery from those bad days is coming about.

7: *1987: Ferrari Loses Its Way*

The year 1987 was Ferrari's 40th in Grand Prix racing and it was to be accompanied by dramatic changes. John Barnard had left McLaren to join Ferrari as Technical Director in November 1986, by when the design of the 1987 car had largely been settled. Bernard's main task, operating from his GTO Limited (Guildford Technical Office), was to assume responsibility for the design and development of a new, very much long-term car for 1989 and the 3500 cc unsupercharged Formula.

The new F1/87 was largely the work of Gustav Brunner, together with Harvey Postlethwaite. The team had also been joined by two experts from Renault, the engine designer Jean-Jacques His and aerodynamicist Jean-Claude Migeot. The design of the new car was clearly influenced by McLaren and Williams.

Powering the F1/87 was a new engine, Ferrari's Tipo 033, a 90-degree V-6. In accordance with the new rules laid down by F.I.S.A., the engine was fitted with provision for a pop-off valve which opened if a pressure of 4-bar boost was exceeded. These valves were distributed at races by F.I.S.A. on a random basis. The new engine was smaller and lighter than its predecessor and incorporated sparking plugs with their own ignition coils (as seen on Renault engines in 1986), thereby doing away with the need for an alternator.

Transmission was by a new 6-speed longitudinal gearbox. The monocoque was much revised and there was double wishbone and pull-rod suspension front and rear, the geometry of which had been influenced by Barnard. In 1987 only Goodyear supplied tyres and by the new arrangement each team was limited to ten sets of tyres per car for each weekend, with only two sets beng allowed in each of the two qualifying sessions. Apart from anything else, this meant the end of qualifying tyres which was no bad thing. As the season progressed Ferrari's collaboration with Goodyear appeared to bring better results in achieving compatibility between suspension set-up and tyres. The F1/87 featured a centre-section and a close-fitting engine cover which were very similar to those of the 1986 Williams, whilst the side-pods also were like those on the Williams. The top and bottom rear bodywork, the rear wing with side-plates and the gearbox cover aped the 1986 McLaren. Although Ferrari made a slow start to the season and the Williams-Honda was to prove the dominant marque, the team took victories in the last two races of the year.

For much of the year Harvey Postlethwaite was conspicuous by his absence from race meetings, whilst the Guildford Office was strongly represented. However, from Hockenheim onwards, Postlethwaite, who was regarded with great affection at the factory and as being to all intents and purposes an 'adopted' Italian, who enjoyed the Italian lifestyle and lived near the factory, came back to races on a regular basis.

It was at Hockenheim that Ferrari introduced aerodynamic changes and it was from this point on in the season that the cars gradually improved, an improvement which was attributed to Postlethwaite's presence by his supporters who included Michele Alboreto. By this time Enzo Ferrari had concluded that John Barnard and his associates should concentrate on the development of the new car whilst the regular team concentrated on the development of the existing car for the remaining 1987 races.

Although Ferrari had dispensed with the services of Stefan Johansson, who had joined McLaren, Alboreto remained with the team and he was joined by Austrian driver, Gerhard Berger. Berger had driven for Arrows in 1985 and switched to Benetton in 1986. With Benetton he had displayed considerable speed and skill, but also the rashness of inexperience. During the year he had won one race, at Mexico City, but on earlier occasions he had revealed his impetuosity by turning up the boost without regard to economy and by jousting for places without too much regard to the outcome. In 1987 Berger was to gain the maturity to match his speed and Ferrari proved to have one of the best driver combinations in Formula 1.

Brazilian Grand Prix

During the year Ferrari raced a total of seven different chassis, producing at Rio 096 for Alboreto, 097 for Berger and 095 as a spare. At Rio, Berger drove the spare car 095. Both drivers were unhappy with their cars in practice, not because there was any shortage of bhp, but rather because of poor engine tuning. Berger was back on the fourth row of the grid with a time of 1 min 30.357 sec, looking nostalgically at the two Benettons of Fabi and Boutsen which had taken places on the second and third rows of the grid! Alboreto was a row behind Berger with 1 min 30.468 sec but the Williams team was all-dominant, with Mansell taking pole position with 1 min 26.128 sec and Piquet alongside him on the grid. Heavy tyre wear on the Rio circuit meant that many drivers made three stops for tyre changes

and Berger finished fourth, on the same lap as Prost's winning McLaren. Alboreto had a miserable race, for he damaged the vertical plates attached to the rear underbody on a kerb and as the race progressed, so they disintegrated, throwing up showers of sparks; the pit called him in for a fourth set of tyres but he plugged on, allowing Berger to go ahead, and spun off on lap 59, although still classified in eighth place.

San Marino Grand Prix

By the Imola race the team had scrapped the vertical plates beneath the rear underbody that had given Alboreto so much trouble in Brazil. There were now sleeves around the rear shock absorbers to protect them from the turbocharger heat. Berger's car had a modified bulkhead so there was more room for his long legs. Both cars showed good speed, but poor reliability in practice. Although suffering from hay fever, puncturing a radiator on debris when Piquet crashed heavily with his Williams on the Friday, and spinning later the same day on oil dropped by Johansson's blown-up McLaren, Berger still managed to take fifth place on the grid in 1 min 27.280 sec. Alboreto was one place slower with a

Ferrari enjoyed mixed fortunes during 1987 but one of the team's better performances earlier in the season was at San Marino where Alboreto finished third behind Mansell (Williams) and Senna (Lotus).

lap in 1 min 28.074 sec, but throughout qualifying he had been plagued by mechanical problems, including a broken gearbox in Friday's untimed session, turbocharger failure on the spare car, a broken constant velocity joint and an engine that cut out during the timed session. However the car was largely sorted by the Saturday when he produced his best time. Alboreto ran steadily in the race, leading briefly when Mansell brought his Williams in for new tyres, and after his own stop for tyres at the end of lap 25, settling down in fourth place, passing Senna's Lotus, being repassed and eventually finishing third behind Mansell (Williams) and Senna (Lotus). Berger pitted at the end of lap 18 complaining that the boost pressure was fading. The mechanics found a broken connector plug in the electronic injection system, but so much time had been lost in investigating the problem that the car was withdrawn.

Belgian Grand Prix

At Spa-Francorchamps there were detail changes only to the Ferraris and this included underbodies with lower mountings on the race cars. That the Ferraris were improving was only too obvious in practice and Berger was fourth fastest overall in 1 min 53.451 sec (compared with Mansell's pole position of 1 min 52.026 sec) and Alboreto turned in fifth fastest time in 1 min 53.511 sec. Streiff (Tyrrell) lost control and hit the barrier at the rise after Eau Rouge and in avoiding Streiff his team-mate Palmer also crashed so the race was stopped. The race was re-started which was a bonus for Berger. He had spun at the so-called 'bus-stop' chicane and collided with Boutsen's Benetton. The cars were refuelled, the race was started from scratch again, and Berger was able to switch to his spare car 095. Berger retired at the end of lap 3 because of piston failure and Alboreto, after running well in second place behind Piquet's Brabham, was eliminated by failure of a constant velocity joint. The McLarens of Prost and Johansson took the first two places.

Monaco Grand Prix

At Monaco Alboreto was entered with 096, and Berger with 097 as usual, but neither driver was to handle his original entry in the race. Here the Ferraris featured a three-piece upper rear wing above a two-piece lower section. Very shortly after the start of the first official qualifying session, Alboreto collided with Christian Danner's Zakspeed on the climb from Sainte Devote to Casino Square. As Alboreto tried to overtake the slower Zakspeed, contact with its left front wheel launched the Ferrari into the barriers and it bounced from barrier to barrier, disintegrating. The Ferrari was completely wrecked, with the gearbox torn off the engine, whilst the Zakspeed was only slightly damaged. The organisers held Danner fully responsible for the accident and disqualified him from the race. It seemed a very harsh decision and a number of informed onlookers, including Senna, who had been following the two cars and nearly collided with the debris, thought that the accident had been Alboreto's fault.

In any event Michele had to take over 098 for the race and qualified fifth in 1 min 26.102 sec. As for Berger, he chose to have his accident once

It was third again for Alboreto at Monaco and here he is seen on the climb up from Sainte Devote.

Three laps before the finish of the 1987 Brazilian Grand Prix Alboreto spun off with his Ferrari F1/87 and was classified eighth. This photograph shows off to good advantage the lines of the 1987 Maranello cars.

1987

In the San Marino Grand Prix at Imola newcomer to the Ferrari team Gerhard Berger retired in sixth place on lap 17 because of electronics problems.

Michele Alboreto retired his Ferrari early in the 1987 Belgian Grand Prix at Spa-Francorchamps because of transmission problems. Here he leads Adrian Campos (Minardi M/187) and Riccardo Patrese (Brabham BT56).

A fine shot of Gerhard Berger and Michele Alboreto with their Ferraris at the Spanish Grand Prix held on the Jerez circuit in September. Neither of the Ferraris was running at the finish, although Alboreto was classified 15th despite retiring because of engine trouble.

115

Right: In the Austrian Grand Prix held in August 1987 Berger retired yet again early in the race, because of turbocharger failure. It was a sad disappointment in his home Grand Prix. Here the sparks fly off the Ferrari's skid plate shortly after the start of the race.

Below: Gerhard Berger scored his second successive win in the 1987 Australian Grand Prix at Adelaide (and Alboreto took second place). It gave Ferrari hopes for 1988 that were not to be fulfilled.

Another view from Monaco in 1987 with Alboreto lapping Ghinzani's Ligier.

Gerhard Berger hard at work at the wheel of his Ferrari at Monaco in 1987.

qualifying on the Thursday was resumed, and he hit the guard rail at the exit of the Esses by the swimming pool. The left front suspension of his Ferrari was written off and he was obliged to switch to spare car 095. During Saturday's practice he was unable to get in a clear lap and eventually took eighth place on the grid in 1 min 26.323 sec. Pole-position man was Mansell with the Williams in 1 min 23.039 sec. The Ferraris ran steadily in the race, benefitting from Prost's blown-up engine, to finish third and fourth behind Senna (Lotus-Honda) who had completely dominated the race and Nelson Piquet (Williams-Honda).

United States (Detroit) Grand Prix

Berger was back at the wheel of 097 which had been rebuilt since Monaco, whilst Alboreto drove 098. The team brought along as spares 095 and 099. Changes to the cars were few, although the team tried a number of different wing arrangements. Nor was practice at Detroit trouble-free, for on the Saturday Gerhard Berger spun into a wall, the result of a faulty rear suspension upright which had made the Ferrari unstable under braking. Alboreto was seventh fastest in 1 min 42.684 sec with Berger two rows back in 1 min 43.816 sec. Mansell took pole position in 1 min 39.264 sec. Berger drove a steady race to finish fourth, but Alboreto was eliminated by gearbox failure on lap 26.

French Grand Prix

At the Paul Ricard circuit Alboreto drove 098, whilst Berger had 099 and the team's spare was 097. As at Detroit the cars were fitted with carbon-fibre clutches and Gleason differentials, although the spare car had a ZF differential on the Friday and Saturday. It was now reckoned that development work on the Ferrari engines meant that they were producing 960 bhp in race trim. A number of different wing configurations were tried on Berger's car. In one sense the team seemed to be progressing backwards, for both Berger and Alboreto were complaining of lack of traction and understeer through the infield loop. Berger was sixth fastest in 1 min 08.198 sec and Alboreto was back a row in 1 min 08.390 sec, both of these times having been set during Friday's practice. In the race the cars ran steadily in fifth and sixth places, but both retired, Alboreto with engine failure and Berger spun off eight laps from the finish because of a broken lug on a suspension upright. The Williams-Hondas of Mansell and Piquet took the first two places.

British Grand Prix

Minor aerodynamic changes characterised the Ferraris at Silverstone where Alboreto drove 098 and Berger 099, whilst the spare 097 featured front suspension of revised geometry. At the rear the suspension had been strengthened where the top link connected to the suspension upright. Both Alboreto and Berger were on the fourth row of the grid, with times of 1 min 09.274 sec and 1 min 09.408 sec, compared with Piquet's pole in 1 min 07.110 sec. Although Alboreto held fifth place in the race, he retired on lap 53 because of damaged suspension. Berger's race was soon over for on lap 8 he spun at the exit of Abbey Curve and scraped the car along the guard rail. The Williams-Hondas of Mansell and Piquet took the first two places.

German Grand Prix

Harvey Postlethwaite returned to the racing circuits at Hockenheim where Ferrari introduced a number of aerodynamic modifications, including a new underbody round the rear wheels, together with a new rear wing with smaller side-plates. There were new gas-filled shock absorbers with twin gas cylinders mounted on top of the gearbox. The second qualifying session on the Saturday afternoon was wet and cloudy, so that almost all the best times were set during Friday afternoon's qualifying. With 097 Berger spun in to the tyre barrier at the right-hand corner after the pits, a result of the left front suspension collapsing as he braked. The cause of the accident was something of a mystery because inspection revealed that the wishbones on that side had buckled, but not broken. Alboreto was fifth fastest in 1 min 43.921 sec, whilst Berger, with the T-car, 099, was tenth fastest in 1 min 45.902 sec. Pole went to Mansell with the Williams-Honda with a lap of 1 min 42.616 sec. Initially in the race Alboreto held fifth place, but at the end of lap 10 he came in to the pits because of fluctuating boost pressure on the left bank of the Ferrari V-6 engine. It was only too obvious that the turbocharger was failing and the car was withdrawn. Berger moved up to seventh place on lap 13, but he retired seven laps later with turbocharger failure. It had been another thoroughly miserable race for Ferrari, whilst Piquet again won for Williams, with Johansson's McLaren second, although he had to limp across the finishing line with a right front wheel falling off the McLaren.

Hungarian Grand Prix

At the Hungarian race there was a new car, 100, for Alboreto, whilst Berger was at the wheel of 098 and the team brought along 097 as a spare. Here the cars ran with the double rear wings, as at Detroit, with vertical fences by the gearbox in carbon-fibre, instead of titanium as previously. As a result of Berger's accident at Hockenheim, the cars featured stiffened wishbones. The turbochargers had been modified following failures on both cars in the German race. During practice the team experimented with a sensor fitted to the gearbox and connected to the electronic control unit, which gave indications of the gear, together with engine revs and so the car's speed. In practice Berger was magnificent, lapping in 1 min 28.549 sec within the last ten minutes of Saturday's qualifying session, and taking a place on the front row of the grid alongside pole position man Mansell who lapped in 1 min 28.047 sec. Remarkably, gone was the lack of traction and Berger was very happy with the car, particularly out of the slower corners. He had very real worries as to whether the car would last the race.

At the Hungaroring the Ferraris of Berger and Alboreto lead Nelson Piquet (Williams FW11B), Ayrton Senna (Lotus 99T), Alain Prost (McLaren MP4/3) and Thierry Boutsen (Benetton B187). Both Ferrari drivers retired and the race was won by Nelson Piquet with Ayrton Senna second.

Alboreto spun in fifth gear in the damp on the Friday, and had another spin after the mechanics had failed to pre-heat his tyres, but took fifth place on the grid in 1 min 30.310 sec.

When the lights turned green for the start, Berger who had anticipated the start slightly, had to steady the Ferrari on the brakes, Mansell sprinted ahead, with Piquet in second place, but Berger drove round the outside of him to take second place at the next left-hand corner. At the end of that first lap the Ferraris were second and third, but Berger was soon out because of differential failure and although Alboreto was now in second place behind Mansell, he had dropped six seconds behind and retired on lap 44 when the engine failed. Piquet (Williams) won the race from Senna (Lotus) and Prost (McLaren).

Austrian Grand Prix

To the Austrian race Ferrari brought 100 for Alboreto with 098 for Berger and 097 as a spare. At the Österreichring the Ferraris had a new sensor to measure turbocharger pressure, but the gearbox sensor had been deleted. The cars featured smaller wings rather similar to those used at Silverstone. The team also had three different engines for qualifying.

Berger was third fastest in practice in 1 min 24.213 sec, whilst Alboreto recorded 1 min 25.077 sec. During practice Berger had been forced to use a spare Ferrari after his own car had developed an engine misfire and at one stage he abandoned the T-car on the circuit with what he thought was electrical trouble — in fact he had inadvertently knocked off the ignition switch. Alboreto suffered a broken exhaust manifold.

After a multiple collision at the start, the race was stopped, the cars were refuelled and the race was started again from scratch. At the restart, Patrese swung right to avoid Mansell and collided with Cheever's Williams. This set off another multi-car accident and the race was again stopped, with ten cars involved in the incident. Alboreto noticed that his steering wheel had not been put on straight and after visiting the pits to put it right he was one of six drivers to start from the pit lane. Initially Berger held third place, but he retired after five laps with a blown turbocharger. Alboreto after his start from the pit lane gradually made up ground to attain fourth place, driving with more fire than he normally displayed, but he retired because of a broken exhaust. This unfortunate race was won by Nigel Mansell (Williams-Honda) who led home his team-mate Piquet with the Benettons of Fabi and Boutsen in third and fourth places.

Gerhard Berger in the Austrian Grand Prix in which he retired early in the race because of turbocharger failure.

Italian Grand Prix

Prior to the Italian race, Ferrari had carried out extensive testing at Imola and the team's main aim was to concentrate on reliability. Apart from engine development, only minor changes had been made to the cars. During testing at Imola, Berger had been fastest and so he arrived on a high note. In both qualifying sessions he was third fastest and his best lap was 1 min 23.933 sec (compared with Piquet's pole in 1 min 23.460 sec), whilst Alboreto was back on the fourth row with a time of 1 min 25.247 sec. During qualifying Alboreto had spun at the second Lesmo turn, hitting the barrier and wrecking the car's right front suspension. He had problems during the second qualifying session with the turbo boost pressure and was unable to lap as fast as he thought the car was capable.

For Alboreto the race was soon over and he retired on lap 14 because of an overheated turbocharger. Despite banging wheels with Mansell at the second of the chicanes, Berger drove a good, steady race to take fourth place behind Piquet (Williams-Honda), Senna (Lotus-Honda) and Mansell (Williams-Honda).

After holding third place in the opening laps of the race, Gerhard Berger eventually finished fourth in the 1987 Italian Grand Prix.

Portuguese Grand Prix

For this race Ferrari brought along 098 for Berger and 100 for Alboreto, with 097 as a spare. Ferrari had been continuing development work on the engines and there were new Garrett turbochargers, not paired right and left, but because of the shortness of time, both were left turbos which meant alterations to the exhaust on the right-hand side to suit the inlet and exit. The team also brought along a complete electronic monitoring system, a first for Ferrari at a race.

The cars ran with double rear wings. At long last the Maranello had sorted out the handling and the Ferraris were running well over Estoril's bumps. Berger enjoyed two days completely trouble-free qualifying and took pole position on the grid in 1 min 17.620 sec, with Mansell (Williams) alongside him in 1 min 17.951 sec. Alboreto's best lap was in 1 min 18.540 sec, good enough for the third row of the grid, but his qualifying was ruined by gearbox problems on his race car and he switched to the spare.

Once again there was a mêlée at the start and the race had to be restarted, but the red flag was not shown until the end of the second lap. Mansell had squeezed past Berger, but Alboreto lost his Ferrari and spun across the front of Piquet. In all 12 cars were involved. Alboreto was forced to transfer to his spare car. At the start Mansell took the lead, but Berger went ahead at the end of that first lap and the Ferrari and the Williams began to pull clear of Senna's Lotus. Mansell retired early in the race with a minor electrical fault. Alboreto overtook Piquet's Williams and moved up into second place behind his teammate. After the tyre changes, Berger still led from Prost and Piquet, but Alboreto retired because of gearbox problems. All the while Prost was pressing Berger, whose tyres were now in bad condition, and on lap 68 under pressure from the McLaren driver, the Austrian spun, recovering to finish second, 20 seconds in arrears. Berger was much criticised in Italy for his mistake, but what was abundantly clear was that the Ferraris were back on the pace and contenders for victory.

Spanish Grand Prix

It was a fraught practice for the Ferraris at Jerez, for Berger, whilst taking third place on the grid in 1 min 23.164 sec, had to revert to the spare car for the race, 097, because of an oil leak on his race car. Alboreto drove 095 that had been brought along for a testing session after the race itself. He had wrecked his own car at a right-hand corner during unofficial practice on the Saturday. His best lap was in 1 min 24.192 sec, good enough for a place on the second row of the grid alongside his team-mate. Early in the race the Ferraris settled down in fifth and sixth positions, with Berger leading Alboreto, but then Alboreto went ahead of the Austrian on lap 13. Alboreto tried desperately to take fourth place from Senna, for whom he has a particular dislike, but Senna was driving faultlessly and never gave a chance to the Italian. Both Ferraris made tyre changes late in the race but neither made it to the finish. Berger ran over a kerb and smashed an oil cooler and retired ten laps from the finish, whilst shortly afterwards Alboreto's engine blew up. The monitoring equipment in the pits had shown that Alboreto had revved his V-6 engine to 14,500 rpm on three occasions when changing down the box! So the engine blow-up was not entirely unexpected. The race was won by Mansell (Williams) from Prost and Johansson with the McLarens.

Mexican Grand Prix

At the Mexican race there was a new car, 101, for Alboreto and development work was still continuing on the Garrett turbochargers with Garrett representatives in the Ferrari pit. Once again Berger was driving superbly, fastest on the Friday and finishing second fastest to Mansell on the Saturday with a time of 1 min 18.426 sec. He tried desperately hard to snatch back pole position, but spun near the end of Saturday qualifying when he left his braking too late. Alboreto was plagued by engine problems and was back in ninth place on the grid with a time of 1 min 19.967 sec. At this race

Goodyear had told the teams that they should be able to run through the race without a tyre change, provided that there was not too much wheelspin and tyre blistering. Although Berger led on the first lap, he was passed by Boutsen (Benetton) and Berger dropped to 1.6 seconds behind. Both Ferraris were in trouble in this race for Alboreto retired on lap 13 with engine failure, believed to be piston trouble, while Berger was out on lap 21, also with engine failure. The race was won by Mansell (Williams) from his team-mate Piquet with Patrese (Brabham) third.

Japanese Grand Prix

For the Japanese race on the Suzuka circuit, there were no important changes to the Ferraris. Postlethwaite was well satisfied with the way the cars were progressing and they were indeed impressive in qualifying. Berger took pole-position on the grid in 1 min 40.042 sec, with, alongside him, Prost in 1 min 40.652 sec. Alboreto was fourth fastest in 1 min 40.984 sec. When the green light came on for the start, Berger accelerated into the lead ahead of Prost and it was a lead that he was destined not to lose throughout the race. At the start Alboreto had clutch problems, stalled the engine and with a push to get him going, started to catch up the field. When Prost punctured his left rear tyre on debris from Alliot's crashed Lola, the Austrian Ferrari driver was

In the Japanese Grand Prix held on the Suzuka circuit Gerhard Berger scored a fine victory from Senna (Lotus) and Johansson (McLaren).

unchallenged. After ten laps he led Boutsen (Benetton) by close to 12 seconds and Boutsen retired shortly afterwards. By lap 21 Alboreto had climbed back to fifth place. At the finish Berger was over 17 seconds ahead of Ayrton Senna (Lotus-Honda) in second place. Alboreto finished fourth. Berger was naturally delighted with his victory and felt that in many ways it compensated for the mistake he made at Estoril when he spun away his lead and it was a victory that Ferrari needed so badly.

Australian Grand Prix

At Adelaide Berger was suffering from a heavy cold, accompanied by a sore throat and ear-ache, but even so he took pole position in 1 min 17.267 sec, whilst Prost (McLaren) alongside him on the grid recorded 1 min 17.967 sec. Alboreto was sixth fastest in 1 min 18.578 sec. The drivers had the same chassis as at Suzuka, and there were changes of a very detail nature only. Berger was still carried away by the wave of euphoria following his success in Japan, and in magnificent form, despite feeling unwell. For the race he switched to the spare chassis because of an engine misfire on his own car. Berger led throughout the race, despite the undertray dragging at one stage, but was pressed hard by Senna

Another Ferrari victory followed in the Australian Grand Prix at Adelaide where Berger scored his second win of the season.

in the second half of the race. Alboreto finished third. However, after the race Senna was disqualified on an objection put in by the Benetton team because of additional brake trunking on the Lotus and Alboreto was elevated to second place.

In the World Championship, Nelson Piquet was clearly the winner with 73 points, to the 61 of Nigel Mansell, 57 of Ayrton Senna and 46 of Alain Prost, with Berger trailing in fifth place with 36 points. Williams dominated the Constructors' Cup completely with a total of 137 points, compared to McLaren with 76, Lotus with 64 and Ferrari with 53. Ferrari had however won the last two races of the year, and the team's prospects for 1988 could hardly look better.

Second place at Adelaide went to Alboreto, followed here by Alain Prost (McLaren MP4/3).

8: *1988: Best of the Rest*

For the last year of the 1.5-litre turbocharged Formula 1 car, F.I.S.A. made two significant changes to the rules, both affecting engines. There was now a boost limitation of 2.5-bar, reduced from 4-bar in 1987 and the fuel tank capacity was reduced from 195 litres to 150 litres. These changes had two major effects. Firstly the bar limitation (1-bar represents ambient atmospheric pressure) resulted in a reduction in bhp and secondly the cars would have to be more economical than previously because race distances had not been reduced.

The almost complete domination of racing by McLaren and Honda meant that the Ferraris were reduced to the best of the rest, a not very significant best when it is borne in mind just how superior the McLarens were. McLaren International under the control of Ron Dennis was superbly organised and it undoubtedly had the best chassis and also it undoubtedly had the best drivers, for McLaren had been able to sign on both Alain Prost and Ayrton Senna for 1988. As a result the Honda company had withdrawn their engines from Williams to supply them to McLaren in place of the TAG engines with which McLaren had been racing since 1983.

It has been stated that Honda was spending US $50 million a year on Formula 1 and if the value of that expenditure is to be justified by results alone, then Williams in 1986 and 1987 and McLaren above all in 1988 have more than justified it. During the year Ron Dennis had said that McLaren was

making history. This was before the Italian Grand Prix which McLaren lost, but the team did win 15 of the 16 World Championship events during the year. If McLaren had not lost at Monza then certainly history would have been made for McLaren would have achieved the unprecedented record of winning all 16 of the year's Championship races. All the year's Championship races have been won by one team alone in the past, by Alfa Romeo in 1950 and by Ferrari in 1952 and indeed during 1952-53 the Tipo 500 Formula 2 Ferraris won 14 World Championship races in succession, but failed in the last race of 1953 where Fangio (Maserati) was the winner.

Before looking at what Ferrari endeavoured to achieve in 1988, it is necessary to look briefly at the other teams. For the second year Lotus were also supplied with Honda engines, but the driver pairings of Nelson Piquet and his lesser team-mate Satoru Nakajima achieved little success as the team simply could not get the cars on the pace. The only other teams to use turbocharged engines during 1988 were Arrows with B.M.W.-derived Megatron engines, which did secure some good places during the year, together with Zakspeed and Osella who could be disregarded. All the other teams used the 3500 cc normally aspirated engines that were to be compulsory in 1989. March with Judd V-8 engines were the sensation of 1988 and scored far greater success than anyone expected, whilst Benetton with the Ford DFR and Williams who also used Judd engines shone occasionally. Both however had major problems during the year.

Ferrari had perhaps the greatest technical resources of any team and, having won the last two races of 1987, started the year as the hot favourite. The Maranello team's slide into mediocrity was rapid and unexpected, possibly influenced by Enzo Ferrari's own lack of effectual policies and of course sadly Ferrari himself died during the year. John Barnard was still concentrating on the normally aspirated V-12 car for 1989 and it was not until the end of May that he had any influence over the development of the 1988 cars. Of the team's original personnel, Piero Lardi-Ferrari had now been removed from the racing programme to a more senior post; Harvey Postlethwaite, responsible for the development of the

modern Ferrari chassis, was to leave the team during the year as were Jean-Jacques His, the engine specialist, and Jean-Claude Migeot, aerodynamicist. It was not until the beginning of July that John Barnard took over technical direction of the team, under Fiat executive Capelli, and Renzetti resumed his original role in charge of the engine programme.

For 1988, perhaps complacently, Postlethwaite and his colleagues relied on the F1/87/88C cars very similar to those raced the previous year, but the engine had been developed by His to run with the new engine restrictions and the 1988 car featured revised aerodynamics that included new front wings and side-pods, smaller inter-coolers, a narrower engine cover, new underbody and redesigned rear wing with smaller side-plates.

Both Berger and Alboreto remained with the team. Throughout the season Berger sustained Ferrari through his enthusiasm, drive and forceful skill, at the same time retaining a strong sense of humour and a balanced approach to the change in Ferrari fortunes. Well aware that he could not beat the McLarens, Berger's aim was to drive as hard as possible, so that if they should fail he would be the driver to benefit. He completely overshadowed Alboreto, who became something of a victim of Ferrari politics, under immense pressure at Maranello to perform well, but always performing consistently. If morale had been better within the Ferrari team, so might well have been the results.

Gerhard Berger hard at work in the Brazilian Grand Prix held on the Autodromo Nelson Piquet where he finished second to Prost's winning McLaren.

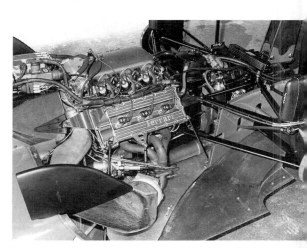

The 1988 Ferrari turbocharged V-6 engine.

Brazilian Grand Prix

During testing before the start of the season Berger had been quickest with his Ferrari at Rio, but when the cars arrived for the Grand Prix the drivers found that the McLaren-Hondas had set new standards and that the Ferraris were well down on power, especially so because the engine department at Maranello had set the electronically controlled wastegate at 2.3-bar which hardly helped the drivers to achieve competitive times. Postlethwaite, too, was full of gloom and despondency, convinced that the chassis was well up to the standards set by McLaren and that the problem was a deficiency in power over which he had no control and Ferrari management seemed unwilling to listen to him. Senna took pole position with his McLaren in 1 min 28.096 sec, whilst Mansell with the Judd-powered Williams which seemed so suited to the Rio circuit was second fastest in 1 min 28.632 sec, with Prost third and Berger taking fourth place on the grid in 1 min 29.026 sec. Alboreto was a row back with a lap in 1 min 30.114 sec.

On the parade lap Senna's McLaren jammed in first gear, delaying the whole field, and after he had lined up on the grid, he threw up an arm and the race was delayed. Into the first corner Prost led, followed by Berger, who had pushed his way past Mansell, and Alboreto held fifth place. Mansell pulled into the pits on lap 19 because of an overheating engine, and whilst he was in the pits the engine stopped and would not restart. Berger stopped on lap 19 for new tyres and rejoined the race in fourth place behind Prost, Senna and Boutsen. Senna was disqualified for changing cars after the green flag had been shown, for according to the stewards the race had been delayed at the start and not stopped and restarted. As Prost only needed one tyre change, once Berger had stopped at the pits for his second change, the outcome of the race was settled. At the finish Berger was just under ten seconds behind Prost, with no hopes of catching the McLaren driver at any stage and Alboreto took fifth place.

San Marino Grand Prix

Since Brazil, only minor modifications had been carried out to the Ferraris, including rear wings of smaller size and a new Magneti-Marelli engine management system (incorporating a sensor that

In the San Marino Grand Prix at Imola in which he finished fifth Berger leads Eddie Cheever (Arrows), Thierry Boutsen (Benetton) and Nigel Mansell (Williams).

opened the wastegate just before the pop-off valve was activated). The team entered 103 for Alboreto and 104 for Berger, as at Rio, and these were to be the usual cars all season. Inevitably the McLarens dominated practice; Berger was back on the third row of the grid, fifth fastest in 1 min 30.683 sec, despite spinning in the wet on the Friday and in the dry on the Saturday, whilst Alboreto was tenth fastest in 1 min 31.520 sec. The Ferraris lack of power compared with the opposition was only too obvious.

Alboreto's clutch dragged as the field moved off on the parade lap, he stalled and had to start from the back of the grid. Senna led throughout the race, Piquet was second for six laps, then Prost took up second postion and that was the finishing order, with Piquet third. Berger finished fifth, a lap in arrears, whilst Alboreto gradually worked his way up with persistency to eighth place, only to have his engine fail six laps from the finish.

Monaco Grand Prix

By Monaco the McLaren domination was becoming almost boring and Senna and Prost took the first two places on the grid, but Berger was third fastest in 1 min 26.685 sec, with Alboreto alongside him in 1 min 27.297 sec. For once the drivers were pleased with their cars, for they felt that there was almost adequate power on this difficult street circuit and that the cars both handled well and were well balanced. At the start Prost missed his change to second gear, Senna took the lead and Berger pushed ahead of the second McLaren to hold position behind the leader. Alboreto was back in fifth place, running steadily behind Mansell. Prost kept trying to force his McLaren past Berger, but on this tight circuit Berger time and time again was able to shut the door. Mansell fell back because of engine overheating and

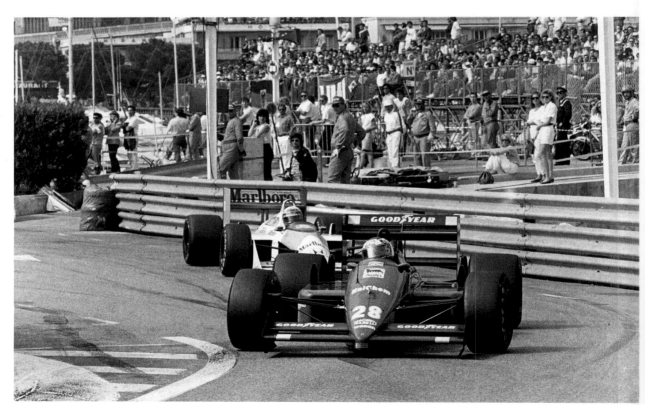

Another second place for Berger followed at Monaco where he is seen leading the winner, the McLaren of Alain Prost.

on lap 33 Alboreto, at the exit from the first chicane at the swimming pool, accelerated hard and tried to force his way past Mansell at the right hand corner that follows. As Mansell took the corner, the left front wheel of the Ferrari struck the right rear of the Williams which was spun into the barrier. By lap 54 the McLarens of Senna and Prost held the first two places ahead of Berger and Alboreto. The outcome of this 78-lap race seemed a foregone conclusion, but on lap 67 Senna made an error at Portier, hitting the inside barrier with the right front wheel then going into the barrier head-on. Prost went on to take his 30th World Championship victory, a little over 20 seconds ahead of Berger, with Alboreto another 20 seconds further in arrears. Certainly for Ferrari it had been the best of the rest.

Mexican Grand Prix

By the Mexican race Ferrari, in their desperate search for power, had made a number of modifications to the engine, including new valves and camshafts and there did seem to be more power available for the drivers. Although Senna and Prost dominated practice, Berger took third place on the grid again in 1 min 18.120 sec, and at times in practice looked as though he might be able to challenge for a place on the front row. Alboreto was fifth fastest in 1 min 19.626 sec, despite an engine failure on the Friday. Prost and Senna took the first two places; until lap nine Berger was boxed in behind Piquet's Lotus and then moved up to third place where he finished the race, too far behind to challenge the McLarens, one place ahead of Alboreto who had moved up a slot following Piquet's retirement with engine problems.

Canadian Grand Prix

There were further engine modifications to the Ferraris at Montreal and the cars now also featured new rear wings and a return to the 1987-style radiators and intercoolers. Again practice was dominated by the McLarens and Berger and Alboreto were third and fourth fastest. Berger's best lap of 1 min 22.719 sec compared with Senna's pole

In the Mexican Grand Prix held on the Autodromo Hermanos Rodriguez the Ferraris finished third and fourth behind the all-conquering McLarens. Here is Berger who took third place.

in 1 min 21.681 sec. Early in the race Berger tried to stay with the flying McLarens, but the more he looked at the readouts from his fuel consumption meter, the more he realised that it was futile. Alboreto was close behind the Austrian, but he was passed by the Benettons of Boutsen and Nannini. Berger's Ferrari retired with an electrical failure and Alboreto's engine blew up. The McLarens took the first two places in the order Senna-Prost, with Boutsen third and Piquet fourth.

United States (Detroit) Grand Prix

The only changes to the Ferraris at Detroit were the adoption of triple-deck rear wings and larger cooling ducts for the rear brakes. For Senna it was to be his sixth consecutive pole position, but both Ferrari drivers were in superb form and took second and third places on the grid, Berger in 1 min 41.464 sec and Alboreto in 1 min 41.700 sec, with Prost pushed back to fourth place. One of the biggest problems at Detroit was a deteriorating track surface which had to be patched using quick-setting concrete. Berger's race was soon over, for after holding second place until lap 6, when he was passed by Prost, he retired out on the circuit with a punctured rear tyre, the result of contact with Boutsen's Benetton. Alboreto's race lasted longer, but was no luckier. He initially held fourth place, before dropping to fifth, was struck by Nannini's Benetton and spun. After a pit stop he began to climb back through the field, reaching seventh place on lap 45 when he spun again and stalled out on the circuit. Senna and Prost took the first two places ahead of Boutsen (Benetton), de Cesaris (Rial) and Palmer (Tyrrell).

French Grand Prix

There were few changes to the cars themselves at the Paul Ricard circuit, other than that the team used smaller rear wings during qualifying, but there were substantial changes within the Ferrari team. Harvey Postlethwaite had made it known that he was

At Detroit Berger was second fastest in practice and looked as if he would give the McLarens a good run for their money, but he was eliminated by a puncture on lap 6 when holding second place.

leaving Ferrari and would be joining the Tyrrell Organisation and so John Barnard was present at Paul Ricard to look after the cars. A day after the race it was announced that Nigel Mansell had decided to leave Williams and would be joining Ferrari in 1989, which meant that Alboreto would have to leave the team.

In practice it was only too evident that the Ferrari tyre wear vastly exceeded that of the McLarens and during qualifying the Ferrari tyres only lasted for about two laps at best. On the Friday afternoon Oscar Larrauri (Euro Brun) baulked Berger, the two cars collided and Berger's left rear tyre was

Gerhard Berger at the wheel of his F1/88C Ferrari in the 1988 Detroit Grand Prix. He retired because of a puncture when holding second place on lap 6. Boutsen (Benetton) had slashed the Ferrari's left rear tyre with right front wing end-plate.

The installation of the turbocharged Ferrari engine in the 1988 chassis.

In the rain-soaked British Grand Prix, Berger led the opening laps from Senna (McLaren) and Alboreto, but the Austrian fell back to sixth place and lost another three places on the last lap as his engine spluttered on the remaining dregs of fuel.

The Ferrari mechanics work on Alboreto's Ferrari during practice for the 1988 German Grand Prix. In this race Alboreto took a sound fourth place.

The Belgian Grand Prix at Spa-Francorchamps proved another disappointing race for the Ferrari team. Here is Alboreto who retired with engine trouble on lap 36 when holding third place.

Just as unfortunate was Berger who retired on lap 12 with electronics problems.

In 1988 the French Grand Prix was held on the very fast Paul Ricard circuit near Marseilles and again the Ferraris proved second best to McLarens in both practice and the race. Alboreto finished third ahead of Berger in this race.

punctured. Berger was third fastest to the McLarens in 1 min 08.282 sec (Prost took pole in 1 min 07.589 sec) and Alboreto, despite lack of grip throughout qualifying, was alongside the Austrian with a lap in 1 min 09.422 sec.

At the start Prost led away from Senna, with Berger pressing hard in third place and Alboreto fourth. On lap 37 Senna passed Prost, but Prost took the lead again on lap 61 and this was the finishing order for the McLaren team. Alboreto went ahead of Berger when Berger ran low on fuel and had to ease back. Alboreto finished third, over a minute behind the winner, and Berger was fourth a lap in arrears, having paid the price for his exuberant press-on driving at the start of the race.

British Grand Prix

At the British race the team adopted a revised engine management system, which, it was hoped, would improve fuel consumption and there were other minor chassis changes. The sensation of practice was the speed of the Ferraris, on a circuit that was ideally suited to their engine characteristics; despite time lost by Berger with gearbox trouble on the Friday, he took pole-position in 1 min 10.133 sec and Alboreto was second fastest in 1 min 10.332 sec. On this circuit the handling of the McLarens was far from good and both were understeering badly. Even so, they occupied the second row of the grid. Race day proved wet and miserable, and with prospects of the rain continuing throughout the race and a great deal of water lying on the track.

At the green light Berger slipped into the lead from Alboreto, both cars enveloped in spray, but on that first lap Senna pushed his McLaren through into second place ahead of Alboreto. Berger still led at the end of the first lap, harried all the way by Senna, but Prost was unhappy with the handling of his car in these conditions and was falling further and further back. On lap 14 at the Woodcote chicane Senna accelerated through the inside to take the lead, whipping past Prost's McLaren which they were just about to lap. Prost decided that the race was quite hopeless and retired at the end of lap 24. As wet lap succeeded wet lap, the Ferrari drivers becoming more and more worried about fuel, Berger managed to

Another view of Alboreto in the French race. This side view shows off the superb lines of the 1988 Ferrari F1/87.

hold on to second place, while Alboreto had slipped back down the field to seventh. At the end of lap 46 Alboreto was called in for slicks but it was a hopeless mistake on this wet circuit which certainly was not going to dry out and after only five more laps, Alboreto stopped again for another set of wet tyres to be fitted. Mansell took Berger for second place on lap 50, Alboreto ran out of fuel on lap 63, two laps before the finish, and on the very last lap Berger's engine misfired on the run-in from Woodcote to the flag. Already back in sixth place, he was passed before the flag by Warwick, Cheever and Patrese to finish ninth. The finishing order behind Senna was Mansell, Nannini (Benetton), Gugelmin (March) and Piquet (Lotus).

German Grand Prix

Not long after the Silverstone race it was announced that engine specialist Jean-Jacques His, who had headed the Formula 1 department at Maranello had left Ferrari to return to Renault. There were few changes to the Ferraris at Hockenheim. On the Friday Berger was travelling flat out in sixth, at something over 190 mph, when he caught Cheever (Arrows) who was about to pass the Euro Brun of Larrauri. Berger reckoned that with two wheels on the grass there was room enough to get by, but the

Arrows swept across the front of the Ferrari taking up most of the track and the Austrian was forced onto the grass with all four wheels; Berger's car spun back across the track between the Euro Brun and the Arrows in a vast cloud of blue tyre-smoke. Despite this drama Berger took third place on the grid in 1 min 46.115 sec with Alboreto alongside him in 1 min 47.154 sec. Inevitably Senna and Prost took the front row with their McLarens. Senna led the race from green light to fall of flag, but Berger held second until lap 12 when Prost brought his McLaren through into second place. With power and fuel limitations, Berger was unable to fight back and at the finish was a little over 50 seconds behind the winner. Alboreto took fourth place after Alessandro Nannini's Benetton stopped at the pits because of throttle problems.

Hungarian Grand Prix

Changes again were few to the Ferraris of the Hungaroring, but there was a new inter-cooler which incorporated an electronic thermostat and by-pass valve. At this race the Ferrari team was a shambles, with the F1/87 cars handling badly, lacking traction and well off the pace. Throughout practice the team tried all sorts of chassis tweaks without success and Berger spun on both qualifying days. He finished up back on the fifth row of the grid with a time of 1 min 29.244 sec, slower not only than the McLarens, but both Williams entries, both March 881s and both Benettons. For Alboreto it was an even more hopeless situation, for his car was running on only five cylinders for much of qualifying and on the Saturday when he took out the T-car, the clutch failed. He was back in 15th place on the grid. John Barnard, the new Technical Director, did not arrive at the race until the Saturday and at once persuaded Gerhard Berger that they should change the chassis settings. Barnard made a substantial number of adjustments to the car and Berger, who always impressed Barnard with his willingness to try something new, was very happy with the much improved handling and balance of his Ferrari. In the race Berger drove with determination and enthusiasm, finishing fourth behind the McLarens of Senna and Prost and Boutsen's Benetton. Alboreto retired his Ferrari when the engine cut out on lap 41; at this time he was holding eighth place.

Belgian Grand Prix

By the Belgian race at Spa-Francorchamps, Ferrari was again the best of the rest. Berger took third place on the grid, inevitably behind the McLarens, with a lap in 1 min 54.581 sec, compared with Senna's pole in 1 min 53.718 sec. During the first day's practice Berger was convinced that, but for trouble with the pop-off valve, he would have been able to mix it with the McLarens; any hopes of doing so on the Saturday were spoilt by the wet weather. Alboreto was fourth fastest in 1 min 55.665 sec, and seemed to revel in lapping in the drizzle on Saturday. He did however spin off causing an early end to the session, but as no worthwhile laps were likely to be recorded no one was too upset. At the start the Ferraris took up third and fourth places, with Berger heading Alboreto, and the Austrian trying hard to snatch second place from Prost. However, there was a problem with the engine and he was in the pits at the end of lap 3; he rejoined the race, setting fastest lap of 128.542 mph but retired. Alboreto retained a lonely third place, but retired seven laps from the finish when the engine blew up.

At the Hungaroring the Ferraris were plagued by lack of grip, but in the race Berger's car incorporated a number of suspension adjustments suggested by John Barnard. In this practice photograph Berger, who finished fourth, leads Nannini (Benetton).

Senna and Prost took the first two places ahead of the Benettons of Boutsen and Nannini.

Italian Grand Prix

At Monza Ferrari was struggling to retain its amour propre in the fact of a home crowd and Alboreto, usually slower than his team mate, took third place on the grid in 1 min 26.988 sec, with Berger alongside him in 1 min 26.654 sec. Inevitably the McLarens occupied the front row of the grid. When the cars were about to leave for the warm-up lap, Berger found that the throttle on his car was sticking, so he switched to spare car, 102. He then learned over the radio that the race car had been repaired and so he got back into that, only to find that the throttle was still sticking. So it was back once more to 102 which he raced. Just as inevitably as Senna led from Prost, so almost inevitably Berger took third place, leading Alboreto who was having problems with fourth gear jumping out; Alboreto eased off to allow the gearbox to cool and this solved

The Italian Grand Prix at Monza was the luckiest race of the year for Ferrari. After both McLarens had been eliminated Berger (see here) and Alboreto delighted the crowd by taking a Maranello 1-2.

the problem. As the race progressed, so Senna extended his lead over Prost and it became noticeable that Prost's engine was sounding flat and that Berger was closing the gap. Berger took second place on lap 35 and on that lap Prost retired in the pits with engine problems.

In the early laps of the race Berger had pressed too hard with the Ferrari and had to ease back to conserve fuel, but now he began to speed up, closing to 8.9 seconds behind Senna at the end of lap 46 — seven laps earlier it had been a 24-second gap. Alboreto too was closing on Berger and set fastest lap of the race in 145.662 mph. Senna had been forced to back off because of the heavy fuel consumption in the opening laps when he had been under pressure from Prost and there seemed a very real risk that his McLaren's fuel would not last the distance. On lap 50, as he approached the chicane, Senna was about to lap the Williams of Schlesser (deputising for Mansell who was unwell); Schlesser had been shown the blue flag and kept well to the right, but locked his brakes and slid straight on so that Senna's right rear wheel rode over the left front wheel of the Williams. Senna spun to a halt on top of the kerb, firmly wedged and unable to rejoin the race. In front of a totally euphoric home crowd Berger won by less than

Alboreto in the Italian Grand Prix.

a second from Alboreto, with the Arrows of Cheever and Warwick in third and fourth places. So Ron Dennis' wish to make history failed and the McLaren record of victories was broken. For Ferrari it was a lucky victory, but Berger had been pressing hard all season waiting for just a moment and Alboreto deserved some consolation before he finally left the Ferrari team.

Portuguese Grand Prix

As Ferrari still struggled to make the cars more competitive, despite this late stage in the season, at Estoril the team was joined by Ing. Dominici, a turbocharger specialist from Fiat. In practice the gathering strength of the normally aspirated cars was only too evident, for whilst Prost and Senna took the first two places on the grid, Ivan Capelli was third fastest in his March-Judd in 1 min 18.812 sec, with Berger in fourth place. Alboreto was plagued by problems during qualifying and he ended up by taking a very disappointing seventh place on the grid in 1 min 19.372 sec.

The McLarens went straight into the lead at the start of the race, Prost ahead of Senna, but the Brazilian was being hounded by the March-Judd of Capelli, with Berger in fourth place and Alboreto some places back. Capelli took second place at the end of lap 21, and the March driver closed up to less than two seconds behind Prost. Berger moved up into third place ahead of Senna under braking for a downhill left-hander on lap 23 and began to close on Capelli, setting fastest lap of 118.722 mph. As he prepared to pass, Berger moved his hand to adjust the ride-height, but by error activated the fire extinguisher button. Cold extinguisher fluid was sprayed round the cockpit, Berger's foot slipped off the brake pedal, he spun and the Ferrari was bogged down in the gravel. By lap 56 Alboreto was in third place behind Prost and Capelli, but although the computer read-out told him that the fuel situation was good, the Ferrari ran out of fuel on the last lap and Alboreto finished fifth behind Prost (McLaren), Capelli (March), Boutsen (Benetton) and Warwick (Arrows). Senna took sixth place in this race, following a pit stop to change tyres because of chronic oversteer.

Spanish Grand Prix

As a result of Berger's misadventure at Estoril, by the Spanish race the Ferrari team had abandoned the front ride-height control. The cars also featured new

rear wings of higher downforce. Again the Ferraris were pushed well down the grid and Berger had not completed a lap during the first practice session before the engine failed. He took over the spare, but had to abandon that because of electrical failure. After all these problems the best he could manage was eighth place on the grid in 1 min 25.46 sec, compared with pole-position man Senna's best lap in 1 min 24.067 sec. Alboreto, after his share of problems including throttle and engine trouble, took tenth place on the grid in 1 min 26.447 sec. It was another miserable race for the team for Alboreto's Ferrari retired with engine trouble on lap 16 and Berger finished a poor sixth, behind Prost (McLaren), Mansell (Williams), Nannini (Benetton), Senna (McLaren) and Patrese (Williams).

A superb view of Berger's Ferrari at the 1988 Spanish Grand Prix held at the Jerez circuit.

Japanese Grand Prix

A year previously, Berger had won at Suzuka, following this up with a victory in Australia, but all the team's hopes and aspirations had turned to ashes and now Berger was struggling hard to be second to the McLarens. Once again Senna and Prost were fastest in practice and which of them won the World Championship was still very much in the balance. On the Friday Berger had been second fastest in practice, but he finished qualifying in third place on the grid, with a lap in 1 min 43.353 sec, over a second slower than Prost who in turn was over half a second slower than pole-position man Senna. Alboreto, trying hard but not achieving much in the way of results took ninth place in 1 min 43.972 sec. After nearly stalling at the start of the race, Senna drove through the field to take the lead, beating Prost into second place, scoring his eighth win of the year and taking his first World Championship. As for the Ferrari drivers, Berger challenged Prost for the lead in the early laps of the race, but fuel consumption was always the bugbear and Berger had to drop back, being passed by Senna and Boutsen to finish fourth. Alboreto had held fourth place on the first lap, but he collided with Nannini on lap 8, spun into the sand, stopped for new tyres and, slowed by fuel economy problems and unhappy with the car's handling, at the flag he was down in 11th place, a lap in arrears.

Australian Grand Prix

It was the same story as before, with Senna taking pole-position and alongside him Prost with the second McLaren. At Adelaide Berger could only manage fourth fastest in 1 min 19.517 sec, 1.8 sec slower than Senna and beaten by Mansell (Williams); Berger freely admitted that he might well have been in third place on the grid but for the number of mistakes he had made, losing precious fractions of a second. For Alberto it was a thoroughly miserable final race with Ferrari. He was quite prepared to tell anyone willing to listen the reasons why, for he was convinced that no one in the Ferrari team was

prepared to help him sort the car out or was taking any interest. For Ferrari the race proved yet another disaster. On only the first lap Alboreto collided with the Dallara of Caffi, went off the track and retired. Prost led from Senna, with Berger pushing hard in third place. With the team's agreement he had decided to turn the boost right up, regardless of fuel consumption and on lap 3 pushed his way through to second place as McLaren and Ferrari banged wheels. He now closed up on Prost and on lap 14 took the lead. During the next 12 laps he extended his lead, but his prospects of finishing the race in any event were slim and on lap 26 he collided with Arnoux' Ligier and both cars were eliminated from the race. Prost and Senna took the first two places.

For McLaren it had been a magnificent season and although history had not been made in the sense tht McLaren's record of wins was unbroken, no team has ever dominated Grand Prix racing so convincingly and to the point where so many spectators complained that racing was plain boring. McLaren won 15 of the year's 16 races, with Senna taking eight victories and Prost seven; in the World Championship Senna scored a total of 94 points (winning the Championship with 90 qualifying points) and whilst Prost's gross total was 105, the qualifying figure was 87 which gave him second place. In the Constructors' Cup McLaren scored the overwhelming total of 199 points. Ferrari was of course the only other team to win a race, the Italian Grand Prix, and so was truly best of the rest. Berger finished third in the World Championship with 41 points and Ferrari took second place in the Constructors' Cup with 65 points.

Post-script

Adelaide had represented the end of the era of the 1000 bhp turbocharged cars and, some would say, was to be followed by a return to sanity in Grand Prix racing. In 1989 Gerhard Berger remained with the team, joined by Nigel Mansell. Alboreto left to drive for the Tyrrell team. At the Brazilian Grand Prix in 1989 the new era opened when Mansell won the race for Ferrari.

Appendix 1

Ferrari Grand Prix Results, 1981 – 88

1981

US Grand Prix West, Long Beach,
15 March, 162.61 miles
Retired, G. Villeneuve (049), drive-shaft
Retired, D. Pironi (050), engine

Brazilian Grand Prix, Rio Autodromo,
29 March, 193.82 miles (race stopped
after two hours)
Retired, G. Villeneuve (051), turbocharger wastegate
Retired, D. Pironi (050), collision with Prost

Argentine Grand Prix, Buenos Aires
Autodromo, 12 April 196.548 miles
Retired, G. Villeneuve (051), drive-shaft
Retired, D. Pironi (050), engine

San Marino Grand Prix, Autodromo
Dino Ferrari, Imola, 3 May, 187.90 miles
5th, D. Pironi (050)
7th, G. Villeneuve (052)

Belgian Grand Prix, Zolder, 17 May,
142.99 miles
4th, G. Villeneuve (052)
8th, D. Pironi (050)

Monaco Grand Prix, Monte Carlo,
31 May, 156.406 miles
1st, G. Villeneuve (052), 82.039 mph
4th, D. Pironi (050), 1 lap in arrears

Spanish Grand Prix, Jarama, 21 June,
164.64 miles
1st, G. Villeneuve (052), 92.682 mph
15th, D. Pironi (053), 4 laps in arrears

French Grand Prix, Dijon-Prenois, 5 July,
188.88 miles
5th, D. Pironi (053), 1 lap in arrears
Retired, G. Villeneuve (052), electrics

British Grand Prix, Silverstone, 18 July,
199.38 miles
Retired, G. Villeneuve (054), accident damage
Retired, D. Pironi (053), engine

German Grand Prix, Hockenheim,
2 August, 189.832 miles
10th, G. Villeneuve (054), 1 lap in arrears
Retired, D. Pironi (053), engine

Austrian Grand Prix, Österreichring,
16 August, 195.686 miles
9th, D. Pironi (051B), 1 lap in arrears
Retired, G. Villeneuve (050B), accident damage

Dutch Grand Prix, Zandvoort,
30 August, 190.229 miles
Retired, G. Villeneuve (050B), accident
Retired, D. Pironi (051B), accident damage

Italian Grand Prix, Monza,
13 September, 187.403 miles
5th, D. Pironi (049B)
Retired, G. Villeneuve (053), turbocharger

Canadian Grand Prix, Île Notre Dame,
27 September, 172.62 miles
3rd, G. Villeneuve (052)
Retired, D. Pironi (049B), engine

Las Vegas Grand Prix, Caesars Palace,
17 October, 170.1 miles
9th D. Pironi (049B), 2 laps in arrears
Disqualified, G. Villeneuve (051B)

1982

South African Grand Prix, Kyalami,
23 January, 196.35 miles
18th, D. Pironi (056), 6 laps in arrears
Retired, G. Villeneuve (055), turbocharger

Brazilian Grand Prix, Rio Autodromo,
21 March, 196.945 miles
6th, D. Pironi (056), 1 lap in arrears
Retired, G. Villeneuve (057), accident

United States Grand Prix West, Long
Beach, 4 April, 160.81 miles
Disqualified, G. Villeneuve (058)
Retired, D. Pironi (056), accident

San Marino Grand Prix, Imola, 25 April,
187.90 miles
1st, D. Pironi (058), 116.63 mph
2nd, G. Villeneuve (059)

Belgian Grand Prix, Zolder, 9 May,
185.38 miles
Non-started, G. Villeneuve (058), fatal accident in practice
Non-started, D. Pironi (059), entry withdrawn

Monaco Grand Prix, Monte Carlo,
23 May, 156.406 miles
2nd, D. Pironi (059), 1 lap in arrears

United States Grand Prix (Detroit),
6 June, 154.566 miles
3rd, D. Pironi (056)

Canadian Grand Prix, Circuit Gilles
Villeneuve, Montreal, 13 June, 191.82
miles
9th, D. Pironi (056/059), 3 laps in arrears

Dutch Grand Prix, Zandvoort, 3 July,
190.228 miles
1st, D. Pironi (060), 116.383 mph
8th, P. Tambay (057), 1 lap in arrears

British Grand Prix, Brands Hatch,
18 July, 198.63 miles
2nd, D. Pironi (060)
3rd. P. Tambay (061)

French Grand Prix, Paul Ricard, 25 July,
194.94 miles
3rd, D. Pironi (060)
4th, P. Tambay (061)

German Grand Prix, Hockenheim,
8 August, 190.055 miles
1st, P. Tambay (061), 130.426 mph

Austrian Grand Prix, Österreichring,
15 August, 190.055 miles
4th, P. Tambay (061)

Italian Grand Prix, Monza,
12 September, 187.403 miles
2nd, P. Tambay (062)
3rd, M. Andretti (061)

Caesars Palace Grand Prix, Las Vegas,
25 September, 170.1 miles
Retired, M. Andretti (061), rear suspension failure.

1983

Brazilian Grand Prix, Rio Autodromo,
13 March, 196.945 miles
5th, P. Tambay (065)
10th, R. Arnoux (064), 1 lap in arrears

United States Grand Prix West, Long
Beach 27 March, 156.625 miles
3rd, R. Arnoux (064)
Retired, P. Tambay (065), accident

Race of Champions, Brands Hatch,
10 April, 104.544 miles
Retired, R. Arnoux (063), engine

French Grand Prix, Paul Ricard, 17 April,
194.95 miles
4th, P. Tambay (062)
7th, R. Arnoux (064), 1 lap in arrears

San Marino Grand Prix, Imola, 1 May,
187.90 miles
1st, P. Tambay (065), 115.251 mph
3rd, R. Arnoux (064), 1 lap in arrears

Monaco Grand Prix, Monte Carlo,
15 May, 156.406 miles
4th, P. Tambay (065)
Retired, R. Arnoux (064), accident

Belgian Grand Prix, Spa-Francorchamps,
22 May, 173.127 miles
2nd, P. Tambay (065)
Retired, R. Arnoux (062), engine

United States (Detroit) Grand Prix,
Detroit, 5 June, 150 miles
Retired, R. Arnoux (064), electrics
Retired, P. Tambay (065), stalled at start

Canadian Grand Prix, Circuit Gilles
Villeneuve, Montreal, 12 June, 191.82
miles
1st, R. Arnoux (064), 106.044 mph
3rd. P. Tambay (065)

British Grand Prix, Silverstone, 16 July,
196.44 miles
3rd, P. Tambay (067)
5th, R. Arnoux (066)

German Grand Prix, Hockenheim,
7 August, 190.055 miles
1st, R. Arnoux (066), 130.813 mph
Retired, P. Tambay (067), engine

Austrian Grand Prix, Österreichring,
14 August, 195.699 miles
2nd, R. Arnoux (068)
Retired, P. Tambay (067), engine

Dutch Grand Prix, Zandvoort,
28 August, 190.228 miles
1st, R. Arnoux (066), 115.640 mph
2nd, P. Tambay (067)

Italian Grand Prix Monza, 11 September,
187.403 miles
2nd, R. Arnoux (068)
4th, P. Tambay (069)

Grand Prix of Europe, Brands Hatch,
25 September, 198.63 miles
9th, R. Arnoux (066) 1 lap in arrears
Retired, P. Tambay (069), accident

South African Grand Prix, Kyalami,
15 October, 196.35 miles
Retired, P. Tambay (069), turbocharger
Retired, R. Arnoux (066), engine

1984
Brazilian Grand Prix, Rio Autodromo,
25 March, 190.692 miles
Retired, M. Alboreto (072), brake caliper failure
Retired, R. Arnoux (073), battery failure

South African Grand Prix, Kyalami,
7 April, 191.247 miles
12th, M. Alboreto (072), 5 laps in arrears, not
running at the finish, electronic ignition
Retired, R. Arnoux (073), fuel injection

Belgian Grand Prix, Zolder, 29 April,
185.38 miles
1st, M. Alboreto (074), 115.221 mph
3rd, R. Arnoux (073)

San Marino Grand Prix, Imola, 6 May,
187.90 miles
2nd, R. Arnoux (073)
Retired, M. Alboreto (074), exhaust

French Grand Prix, Dijon-Prenois,
20 May, 186.535 miles
4th, R. Arnoux (073)
Retired, M. Alboreto (074), engine failure

Monaco Grand Prix, Monte Carlo,
3 June, 63.797 miles (rain stopped race)
4th, R. Arnoux (074)
7th, M. Alboreto (075), one lap in arrears

Canadian Grand Prix, Circuit Gilles
Villeneuve, 17 June, 191.82 miles
5th, R. Arnoux (075) 2 laps in arrears
Retired, M. Alboreto (076), engine failure

United States (Detroit) Grand Prix,
24 June, 157.500 miles
Retired, M. Alboreto (076), engine failure
Retired. R. Arnoux (075). accident

United States (Dallas) Grand Prix, 8 July,
162.408 miles
2nd, R. Arnoux (075)
Retired, M. Alboreto (076), accident

British Grand Prix, Brands Hatch,
22 July, 185.566 miles
5th, M. Alboreto (076), 1 lap in arrears
6th, R. Arnoux (075), 1 lap in arrears

German Grand Prix, Hockenheim,
5 August, 185.83 miles
6th, R. Arnoux (075), 1 lap in arrears
Retired, M. Alboreto (072), engine misfire

Austrian Grand Prix, Österreichring,
19 August, 188.313 miles
3rd, M. Alboreto (076)
7th, R. Arnoux (077), 1 lap in arrears

Dutch Grand Prix, Zandvoort,
26 August, 187.586 miles
13th, R. Arnoux (075)†, 5 laps in arrears, not
running at finish, electrics
Retired, M. Alboreto (076), engine

Italian Grand Prix, Monza, 9 September,
183.801 miles
2nd, M. Alboreto (076)
Retired, R. Arnoux (077), gearbox

European Grand Prix, Nürburgring,
7 October, 189.091 miles
2nd, M. Alboreto (074)
5th, R. Arnoux (077)

Portuguese Grand Prix, Estoril,
21 October, 189.207 miles
4th, M. Alboreto (074)
9th, R. Arnoux, (077), 1 lap in arrears

1985
Brazilian Grand Prix, Rio Autodromo,
7 April, 190.692 miles
2nd, M. Alboreto (079)
4th, R. Arnoux (080), 2 laps in arrears

Portuguese Grand Prix, Estoril, 21 April,
181.098 miles
2nd, M. Alboreto (079)
8th, S. Johansson (080), 5 laps in arrears

San Marino Grand Prix, Imola, 5 May,
187.90 miles
6th, S. Johansson (079), 3 laps in arrears, not
running at the finish, fuel
Retired, M. Alboreto (081), electrics

Monaco Grand Prix, Monte Carlo,
19 May, 160.522 miles
2nd, M. Alboreto (081)
Retired, S. Johansson (079), accident

Canadian Grand Prix, Circuit Gilles
Villeneuve, 16 June, 191.82 miles
1st, M. Alboreto (081), 108.544 mph
2nd, S. Johansson (082)

United States (Detroit) Grand Prix,
Detroit, 23 June, 157.500 miles
2nd, S. Johansson (082)
3rd, M. Alboreto (081)

French Grand Prix, Paul Ricard, 7 July,
191.337 miles
4th, S. Johansson (081)
Retired. M. Alboreto (079). turbocharger

British Grand Prix, Silverstone, 21 July,
190.580 miles (race scheduled for
193.512 miles, but stopped one lap
early by error)
2nd, M. Alboreto (081), 1 lap in arrears
Retired, S. Johansson (079), accident

German Grand Prix, Nürburgring,
4 August, 189.091 miles
1st, M. Alboreto (080) 118.773 mph
9th, S. Johansson (079), 1 lap in arrears

Austrian Grand Prix, Österreichring,
18 August, 191.993 miles
3rd, M. Alboreto (080)
4th, S. Johansson (079)

Dutch Grand Prix, Zandvoort,
25 August, 184.944 miles
4, M. Alboreto (080)
Retired, S. Johansson (079), engine

Italian Grand Prix, Monza, 8 September,
183.801 miles
5th, S. Johansson (083), 1 lap in arrears
13th, M. Alboreto (085), 6 laps in arrears, not
running at the finish, engine

Belgian Grand Prix, Spa-Francorchamps,
15 September, 185.669 miles
Retired, M. Alboreto (085), clutch
Retired, S. Johansson (083), engine

European Grand Prix, Brands Hatch,
6 October, 196.050 miles
Retired, M. Alboreto (085), turbocharger
Retired, S. Johansson (086), electrics

South African Grand Prix, Kyalami,
19 October, 191.247 miles
4th, S. Johansson (086), 1 lap in arrears
Retired, M. Alboreto (083), turbocharger

Australian Grand Prix, Adelaide,
3 November, 192.498 miles
5th, S. Johansson (086) 1 lap in arrears
Retired, M. Alboreto (083), gear-linkage

1986
Brazilian Grand Prix, Rio Autodromo,
23 March, 190.692 miles
Retired, M. Alboreto (088), fuel pump
Retired, S. Johansson (087), brakes

Spanish Grand Prix, Jerez, 13 April,
188.708 miles
Retired, M. Alboreto (088), wheel bearing
Retired, S. Johansson (087), brakes, accident

San Marino Grand Prix, Imola, 27 April,
187.90 miles
4th, S. Johansson (090), 1 lap in arrears
10th, M. Alboreto (088), 4 laps in arrears, not
running at the finish, turbocharger failure

Monaco Grand Prix, Monte Carlo,
11 May, 161.298 miles
10th, S. Johansson (090), 3 laps in arrears
Retired, M. Alboreto (088), turbocharger failure

Belgian Grand Prix, Spa-Francorchamps,
25 May, 185.429 miles
3rd, S. Johansson (090)
4th. M. Alboreto (089)

Canadian Grand Prix, Circuit Gilles
Villeneuve, 15 June, 189.07 miles
8th, M. Alboreto (092), 1 lap in arrears
Retired, S. Johansson (091), accident

United States (Detroit) Grand Prix,
Detroit, 22 June, 157.500 miles
4th, M. Alboreto (092)
Retired, S. Johansson (086), electrics

French Grand Prix, Paul Ricard, 6 July,
189.543 miles
8th, M. Alboreto (092), 2 laps in arrears
Retired, S. Johansson (093), turbocharger

British Grand Prix, Brands Hatch,
13 July, 196.050 miles
Retired, M. Alboreto (092), turbocharger
Retired, S. Johansson (093), radiator

German Grand Prix, Hockenheim,
27 July, 185.83 miles
11th, S. Johansson (093), 3 laps in arrears, not
running at the finish, broken rear wing
Retired, M. Alboreto (092), broken differential

Hungarian Grand Prix, Hungaroring,
10th August, 189.557 miles
4th, S. Johansson (090), 1 lap in arrears
Retired, M. Alboreto (092), accident

Austrian Grand Prix, Österreichring,
17 August, 191.993 miles
2nd, M. Alboreto (092), 1 lap in arrears
3rd, S. Johansson (089), 2 laps in arrears

Italian Grand Prix, Monza, 7 September,
183.801 miles
3rd, S. Johansson (093)
Retired, M. Alboreto (092), engine

Portuguese Grand Prix, Estoril,
21 September, 189.207 miles
5th, M. Alboreto (092), 1 lap in arrears
6th, S. Johansson (093), 1 lap in arrears

Mexican Grand Prix, Autodromo
Hermanos Rodriguez, 12 October,
186.801 miles
12th, S. Johansson (092), 4 laps in arrears, not
running at the finish, turbocharger
Retired, M. Alboreto (093), turbocharger

Australian Grand Prix, Adelaide,
26 October, 192.498 miles
3rd, S. Johansson (094), 1 lap in arrears
Retired, M. Alboreto (089), start-line accident

1987
Brazilian Grand Prix, Rio Autodromo,
12 April, 190.692 miles
4th, G. Berger (095)
8th, M. Alboreto (096), 3 laps in arrears, not
running at the finish, spun off

San Marino Grand Prix, Imola, 3 May,
185.30 miles
3rd, M. Alboreto (096)
Retired, G. Berger (097), electronics

Belgian Grand Prix, Spa-Francorchamps,
17 May, 185.429 miles
Retired, M. Alboreto (096), transmission
Retired, G. Berger (095), turbocharger

Monaco Grand Prix, Monte Carlo,
31 May, 161.298 miles
3rd, M. Alboreto (098)
4th, G. Berger (095), 1 lap in arrears

United States (Detroit) Grand Prix,
21 June, 157.500 miles
4th, G. Berger (097)
Retired, M. Alboreto (098), gearbox

French Grand Prix, Paul Ricard, 5 July,
189.543 miles
Retired, G. Berger (099), spun off as result of
suspension failure
Retired, M. Alboreto (098), engine

British Grand Prix, Silverstone, 12 July,
192.985 miles
Retired, M. Alboreto (098), rear suspension
Retired, G. Berger (099), spun off

German Grand Prix, Hockenheim,
26 July, 185.83 miles
Retired, G. Berger (099), turbocharger
Retired, M. Alboreto (098), turbocharger

Hungarian Grand Prix, Hungaroring,
9 August, 189.557 miles
Retired, M. Alboreto (100), engine
Retired, G. Berger (098), differential

Austrian Grand Prix, Österreichring,
16 August, 191.993 miles
Retired, M. Alboreto (100), broken exhaust
Retired, G. Berger (097), turbocharger

Italian Grand Prix, Monza, 6 September,
180.197 miles
4th, G. Berger (098)
Retired, M. Alboreto (100), turbocharger

Portuguese Grand Prix, Estoril,
21 September, 189.207 miles
2nd, G. Berger (098)
Retired, M. Alboreto (097), transmission

Spanish Grand Prix, Jerez,
27 September, 188.708 miles
15th, M. Alboreto (095), 5 laps in arrears, not
running at the finish, engine
Retired, G. Berger (097), damaged oil cooler

Mexican Grand Prix, Autodromo
Hermanos Rodriguez, 18 October,
173.065 miles
Retired, G. Berger (098), engine
Retired, M. Alboreto (101), engine

Japanese Grand Prix, Suzuka,
1 November, 185.670 miles
1st, G. Berger (098), 119.829 mph
4th, M. Alboreto (101)

Australian Grand Prix, Adelaide,
15 November, 192.454 miles
1st, G. Berger (097), 102.299 mph
2nd, M. Alboreto (101)

1988
Brazilian Grand Prix, Rio Autodromo,
3 April, 187.566 miles
2nd, G. Berger (104)
5th, M. Alboreto (103)

San Marino Grand Prix, Imola, 1 May,
187.902 miles
5th, G. Berger (102), 1 lap in arrears
18th, M. Alboreto (103), 6 laps in arrears, not
running at the finish, engine

Monaco Grand Prix, Monte Carlo,
15 May, 161.298 miles
2nd, G. Berger (104)
3rd, M. Alboreto (103)

Mexican Grand Prix, Autodromo
Hermanos Rodriguez, 29 May, 184.054
miles
3rd, G. Berger (104)
4th, M. Alboreto (103), 1 lap in arrears

Canadian Grand Prix, Circuit Gilles
Villeneuve, 12 June, 188.21 miles
Retired, G. Berger (104), electrics and engine
Retired, M. Alboreto (103), engine

United States (Detroit) Grand Prix,
19 June, 157.500 miles
Retired, M. Alboreto (103), accident
Retired, G. Berger (104), puncture

French Grand Prix, Paul Ricard, 3 July,
189.543 miles
3rd M. Alboreto (103)
4th, G. Berger (104), 1 lap in arrears

British Grand Prix, Silverstone, 10 July,
192.985 miles
9th, G. Berger (104), 1 lap in arrears
17th, M. Alboreto (103), 3 laps in arrears, not
running at the finish, run out of fuel

German Grand Prix, Hockenheim,
24 July, 185.83 miles
3rd, G. Berger (104)
4th, M. Alboreto (103)

Hungarian Grand Prix, Hungaroring,
7 August, 189.557 miles
4th, G. Berger (104)
Retired, M. Alboreto (103), engine cut out

Belgian Grand Prix, Spa-Francorchamps,
28 August, 185.429 miles
Retired, M. Alboreto (103), engine
Retired, G. Berger (104), electronics

Italian Grand Prix, Monza,
11 September, 183.801 miles
1st G. Berger (102), 142.000 mph
2nd, M. Alboreto (103)

Portuguese Grand Prix, Estoril,
25 September, 189.207 miles
5th, M. Alboreto (103)
Retired, G. Berger (104), spun off

Spanish Grand Prix, Jerez, 2 October,
188.708 miles
6th, G. Berger (104)
Retired, M. Alboreto (103), engine

Japanese Grand Prix, Suzuka,
30 October, 185.670 miles
4th, G. Berger (104)
11th, M. Alboreto (103), 1 lap in arrears

Australian Grand Prix, Adelaide,
13 November, 192.498 miles
Retired, G. Berger (104), collision with Arnoux
Retired, M. Alboreto (103), accident

Appendix 2

Specifications of Ferrari Grand Prix Cars, 1981-88

It should be noted that all power outputs are estimates and relate to the cars in race rather than qualifying trim.

Model	126C	126C	126C2/B	126C3	126C4
Year raced	1981	1982	1983	1983*	1984
Number Built	6 (049-054*)	10 (055-064*)	4 (062-065*)	4 (066-069)	8 (070-077)
Engine layout	120-degree V-6	120-degree V-6	120-degree V-6	120-degree V-6	120-degree V-6
Capacity (bore and stroke)	1496 cc (81 x 48.4 mm)	1496 cc (81 x 48.4 mm)	1496 cc (81 x 48.4 mm)	1496 cc (81 x 48.4 mm)	1496 cc (81 x 48.4 mm)
Turbocharger	KKK (two)	KKK (two)	KKK (two)	KKK (two)	KKK (two)
Fuel Injection	Lucas/Ferrari	Lucas/Ferrari	Lucas/Ferrari	Lucas/Ferrari	Lucas/Ferrari and Weber/Marelli
Ignition	Magneti Marelli	Magneti Marelli	Magneti Marelli	Magneti Marelli	Magneti Marelli
Bhp at rpm	560 bhp at 11,500 rpm	580 bhp at 11,800 rpm	620 bhp at 11,500 rpm	620 bhp at 11,500 rpm	680 bhp at 11,500 rpm
Transmission	5-speed	5-speed	5-speed	5-speed	5-speed
Front Suspension	Upper rocker arms, lower wishbones, inboard coil spring/damper units	Upper rocker arms, lower wishbones, inboard coil spring/damper units**	Double wishbones, pull-rods, inboard coil spring/damper units	Double wishbones, pull-rods, inboard coil spring/damper units	Double wishbones, pull-rods, inboard coil spring/damper units
Rear Suspension	Upper rocker arms, lower wishbones, inboard coil spring/damper units	Upper rocker arms, lower wishbones, inboard coil spring/damper units	Double wishbones, pull-rods, inboard coil spring/damper units	Double wishbones, pull-rods, inboard coil spring/damper units	Double wishbones, pull-rods, inboard coil spring/damper units
Wheelbase	107.1/112.2 in (2720/2850 mm)	104.6/110.55 in (2657/2808 mm)	104.6 in (2657 mm)	102.4 in (2600 mm)	102.4 in (2600 mm)
Front track	66.93/68.89 in (1700/1750 mm)	70.35 in (1787 mm)	70 in (1780 mm)	70.5 in (1790 mm)	70.5 in (1790 mm)
Rear track	63.8 in (1620 mm)	64.72 in (1644 mm)	64.7 in (1644 mm)	64.7 in (1644 mm)	64.7 in (1644 mm)
	*049 first appeared in 1980	*Also rebuilt 049B, spare car at Kyalami	*Rebuilt 1982 cars	*First appeared at British Grand Prix	
		**Wishbones and pull-rods adopted during the year			

	156/85	F1/86	F1/87	F1/87/88C
Model	156/85	F1/86	F1/87	F1/87/88C
Year raced	1985	1986	1987	1988
Number Built	8 (078-086)	8 (087-094)	7 (095-101)	3 (102-104*)
Engine layout	120-degree V-6	120-degree V-6	90-degree V-6	90-degree V-6
Capacity (bore and stroke)	1496 cc (81 x 48.4 mm)	1496 cc (81 x 48.4 mm)	1496 cc (81 x 48.4 mm)	1496 cc (81 x 48.4 mm)
Turbocharger	KKK (two)	Garrett (two)	Garrett (two)	Garrett (two)
Fuel Injection	Weber/Marelli	Weber/Marelli	Weber/Marelli	Weber/Marelli
Ignition	Magneti Marelli	Magneti Marelli	Magneti Marelli	Magneti Marelli
Bhp at rpm	780 bhp at 12,000 rpm	850 bhp at 11,000 rpm	960 bhp at 11,500 rpm	980 bhp at 11,500 rpm
Transmission	5-speed	5-speed	6-speed	6-speed
Front Suspension	Double wishbones, pull-rods, inboard coil spring/damper units	Double wishbones, pull-rods, inboard coil spring/damper units	Double wishbones, pull-rods, inboard coil spring/damper units	Double wishbones, pull-rods, inboard coil spring/damper units
Rear Suspension	Double wishbones, pull-rods, inboard coil spring/damper units	Double wishbones, pull-rods, inboard coil spring/damper units	Double wishbones, pull-rods, inboard coil spring/damper units	Double wishbones, pull-rods, inboard coil spring/damper units
Wheelbase	102.4 in (2600 mm)	110.9 in (2816 mm)	110.2 in (2800 mm)	110.2 in (2800 mm)
Front track	70.5 in (1790 mm)	70.7 in (1795 mm)	70.7 in (1795 mm)	70.7 in (1795 mm)
Rear track	64.7 in (1644 mm)	65.5 in (1663 mm)	65.7 in (1668 mm)	65.7 in (1668 mm)

*Also raced 101 built in 1987

143

Appendix 3

The Turbocharged Engine

The concept of using the exhaust gases of an internal combustion engine to energize an air compressor, boosting the engine's induction was the invention of a Swiss engineer Alfred Büchi in the early years of the 20th Century. Aviation engine designers adopted turbocharging to maintain intake manifold pressure at high altitude and over the last twenty years many light aircraft with piston engines have used turbochargers, as well as commercial aircraft. During the late 1950s and the early 1960s turbocharging was adopted to provide additional power from diesel engines in heavy commercial vehicles. It was in the late 1960s that turbocharged engines were adopted in Indy cars in the United States and in Europe Renault became very much the pioneer in the late 1970s. The big advantage over supercharging was that with a conventional Roots-type supercharger around 70 bhp could be absorbed in engine power just to drive it. In contrast, the turbocharger is driven by back-pressure in the exhaust manifold.

In essence a turbocharger consists of a small centrifugal compressor, with a radial-inflow turbine which is mounted on a common axial shaft and driven by the exhaust gases. Both the compressor and the radial-inflow turbine are mounted within their own casings. The radial-inflow drive turbine works in conditions of 1000 degrees Centigrade plus in the exhaust gas flow. The exhaust gas speed in relation to the compressor is controlled by the turbine entry nozzle. A diaphragm valve, known as the wastegate, enables excess boost pressure to be bled away to the atmosphere and maintain constant optimum pressure in the induction system. The designer will endeavour to match the turbocharger to the wastegate so the desired boost level is maintained as constantly as possible on any circuit. However at corners where the throttle has to be lifted off to the extent that there is insufficient exhaust gas energy to keep the turbine spinning fast, opening the throttle once more will not immediately speed up the turbine because of the inertia of the rotor assembly. This throttle lag has always provided one of the biggest problems with turbocharged engines. The problem was partly solved by reducing the rotating turbocharger mass to a minimum, by lightening so far as possible the turbine wheels and arranging extra fuel flow when the throttle was first opened.

Because the regulations required that a turbocharged engine would have a maximum capacity of 1500 cc, for these units to be competitive, power had to be well over twice that of a 3-litre unit and by 1983, the year when most teams made pit stops during the race to take on extra fuel (there being no capacity limit other than the tank size) the boost was often turned high for certainly part of the race, and, during the turbocharged years, always during qualifying. So if 3.5 bar (that is 3½ times atmospheric pressure) boost was used, power output in qualifying from a turbocharged engine could be well over 750 bhp in qualifying and over 700 bhp in the race. Most manufacturers were cagey about the actual power output developed at that time, but in late 1983 B.M.W. were admitting to 740 bhp in the later races during the season.

Intercoolers, radiator cores containing hot air under pressure and cooling the car by the passage of the airstream, were used to recover some of the density of the pressurised air from the turbocharged compressor which had lost density when the air was heated by its compression. Because maximum performance from a turbocharged engine is achieved by running it at a critical temperature at all times, the use of intercoolers in a precise and controllable manner became vital. Ferrari (and Renault) also used a system of water-injection which increased further the density of the incoming charge. B.M.W. rejected this approach, as they believed it to be a breach of the regulations in that it involved the use of a banned additive.

Following the ban on refuelling pit stops from 1984 onwards and a fuel limit of 220 litres, fuel management systems became of vital importance to all the teams. In achieving the correct balance between fuel consumption, temperature control and bhp, the TAG turbocharged engine using the MS3 system developed by Porsche and Bosch was so successful that it gave the McLarens a decided advantage. Constant development resulted in the dominant engine becoming the Honda V-6, used initially by Williams and Lotus, and finally by McLaren. By the end of the turbocharged cars in 1988, certain engines were developing close to 1000 bhp, top speeds were in excess of 200 miles an hour and the cars lacked traction to match their power. It was a race in which Ferrari slipped behind, unable to match the Honda engines in terms of either power or fuel consumption.

For a full account of the development of turbocharged engines in Grand Prix racing the reader is referred to *The 1000 BHP Grand Prix Cars* by Ian Bamsey (Haynes, 1988).